A ship goes _____ lifeboat washing ash_____ _____sland. A tribe of cannibals capture ____ and tie him to a stake. For the next several weeks, they proceed to nick him with their spears and drink his blood. Finally, he can't take it any more. He calls the chief and says, "Let me go or kill me, but this has got to stop. I'm tired of being stuck for the drinks."

***

In Cairo, a camel strides into a bar with an Egyptian mummy riding on its back. The camel kneels down, and the mummy crawls off and makes his way to the bar. "What will you have?" asks the bartender. "Nothing for me," says the mummy, "I just came in here to unwind."

***

In the remote Outback of Australia a tough looking guy swaggers into a pub, with a crocodile on a string. The bar clears out when the customers spot the huge reptile. "Do you serve Americans?" growls the man. "We serve anyone," answers the bartender. "Good," says the man. "I'll have a beer and an American for my crocodile."

500 GREAT
BARTENDER'S JOKES

500 GREAT BARTENDER'S JOKES

by

Karen Warner

A SIGNET BOOK

SIGNET
Published by the Penguin Group
Penguin Books USA Inc., 375 Hudson Street,
New York, New York 10014, U.S.A.
Penguin Books Ltd, 27 Wrights Lane,
London W8 5TZ, England
Penguin Books Australia Ltd, Ringwood,
Victoria, Australia
Penguin Books Canada Ltd, 10 Alcorn Avenue,
Toronto, Ontario, Canada M4V 3B2
Penguin Books (N.Z.) Ltd, 182–190 Wairau Road,
Auckland 10, New Zealand

Penguin Books Ltd, Registered Offices:
Harmondsworth, Middlesex, England

First published by Signet, an imprint of New American Library,
a division of Penguin Books USA Inc.

First Printing, January, 1993
10 9 8 7 6 5 4 3 2 1

REGISTERED TRADEMARK—MARCA REGISTRADA

Printed in the United States of America

This book is dedicated to my wonderful,
witty friends and family.

ACKNOWLEDGMENTS

A special word of thanks to all the funny folks—bartenders and otherwise—who contributed their support and their favorite jokes to this book.

Donna Alarie
Robert V. Allen
Chris Ally
Charles Barnard
Susie and Craig Bashel
John W. Bell
Joel Berge
Ernie Bilko
Patti Breitman
Linda Key Bristow
Andy Brock
Michele Canning
John Cantu
Mary Ellen Collins
Diane and Brian
  Conway
J. Spencer Curry
John D'Anneo
Allen Droyan
Bridget Dubriwnny
Will Dunne
Marilyn Fisher
Sam Goldsmith
David W. Greene
Ray Hendess

Mike Iapoce
Russ Johnson
Ken Kitch
Peg and Ernie Kolb
Bonnie and Tommy
  Kole
Adele, Jack, and
  Macklin Kowal
Christine Kowal
Pat Kowal and Ken West
Gayle, Pete, and Katie
  Kowal
Peter Kowal, Jr.
Shirely Kowal
Augi Lamia
Coleen and Chris
  Martin
Tim McCarthy
Currie McLaughlin
Robert Merryman
Susan Miller
Sally and Jack Morley
Mops Morrison
Jim Nichols
George Orteig

Marsha Polk-Townsend
Catherine Pogre
Dave Ratto
Peggy and Bob Regnier
Ted Ring
Stan Rosenfeld
Juanita Rusev
Susan Santos
Carol Shoup-Sanders
Joe Smith
Jill, Zachary, and
   Mackenzie Stanley
Don Stevens
Pat Tierney
Patrick W. Tierney Jr.
Tony von Baeyer
Joe Weatherby
Bill Wilson
Jonathan Yorba

CONTENTS

INTRODUCTION

Feel confident that within these pages you'll find a good number of jokes that are guaranteed to generate laughs. If you are a novice, you will find enough material to fill your personal well of premium jokes. A professional? You can add fresh ammo to your arsenal of surefire laugh getters, or you can find some new gems to replace those jokes that have been told once too often.

Blend these winning jokes with a few simple joke-telling techniques and use our suggested resources for a never-ending supply of humor. In time, your guests will think you are a natural-born comedian.

We recommend that you thumb through a few pages each day rather than read the entire book in one sitting. Reading a joke book is like drinking a fine glass of brandy. One should savor it slowly, a sip at a time.

How to Tell a Joke

You hold in your hand a book that contains hundreds of jokes and stories to make your guests laugh. But a joke is just part of what it takes. A joke doesn't do you any good unless you know how to tell it. It has to be blended with the proper joke-telling techniques to be fully appreciated.

The most expensive gin, the driest vermouth, and the best olives won't make a great martini unless you know how to mix the ingredients properly, and a joke, no matter how funny, won't have the full effect unless it is delivered with finesse.

We list the basic joke-telling techniques used by professionals that will teach you how to deliver the setup and punch line to make your friends laugh out loud.

Use the Right Word

If your guest ordered a vodka on the rocks and you were out of vodka, would you substitute peppermint schnapps because they are both clear and colorless? Of course not. You select the appropriate liquor when making a cocktail; the same principle holds true when telling a joke. You must use the right word or words to perfect your joke. There is the right word and the almost right word.

This is a classic example of how the almost right words can weaken the impact of a good joke: "The other night I was watching the *boxing match* when a hockey game broke out." This is how comedian Rodney Dangerfield tells the joke, "The other night I was watching the *fight* when a hockey game broke out."

Boxing match and *fight* are synonyms, but the right word for this joke is *fight* since the joke's humor comes from a switch on the familiar phrase "A fight broke out at the hockey game" and not "A boxing match broke out at the hockey game."

Jokes are logical, they are worded in a precise

manner. Often one critical misused word, no matter how similar, can throw off the meaning of the joke.

Put the Punch Line at the End

Any bartender will tell you that when making an Irish coffee, the whipped cream is added at the end—it's the last step. And with a well-told joke the final step is telling the punch line. Seems obvious, doesn't it? But often this very basic joke-telling principle is violated.

This joke will show you what we mean: "A CEO was in the hospital recovering from surgery. He received a telegram from the board of directors that read, 'By a vote of four to three, we wish you a speedy recovery.'"

That's a funny story, but it has more punch this way: "A CEO was in the hospital recovering from surgery. He received a telegram from the board of directors that read, 'We wish you a speedy recovery . . . by a vote of four to three.'"

This joke works both ways, but it is a much stronger joke with the punch line "by a vote of four to three" at the end.

Another common mistake is to add unnecessary words after you have delivered the punch line. Compare these two versions of the same joke.

Version One: "The first thing they teach you in medical school is how to check a pulse. The second thing they teach is how to check a credit rating to see if the patient can pay." Version Two: "The first thing they teach you in medical school is how to check a pulse. The second thing they teach is how to check a credit rating." In the first version, the words "to see if the patient can pay" are redundant. Make sure you don't add extra words after you have told the punch line.

Remember the golden rule of joke telling: When telling a joke, make sure the punch line is the last thing you say.

The Personal Touch

When you talk with friends at the bar, you chat about the day's weather, the big game last night, or what the mayor said at a press conference. Your guests are interested in local affairs, not what's going on in the next town. And when you tell a joke, your listeners will laugh harder if the joke is about their town, their sports team, or their local politicians. When you can, tie your jokes in to your guest's frame of reference. Adapt your story to people and places that have a direct connection with either you or your guests. This may be easier than you think. Here's a story from a joke book followed by our personalized version of the same joke.

The scene: "An elderly couple in a restaurant. The waitress, noticing that the man is eating but not the woman, says, 'Aren't you hungry?' The old lady smiles a toothless smile and says, 'Yes, but I'm waiting for Pa to finish with the teeth.' "

Here's how you could rewrite this joke: "I was tending bar and I noticed an elderly couple. The man was eating all the pretzels, but the woman didn't touch one. So I said, 'Excuse me, ma'am, would you like a pretzel?' She smiled at me with a toothless grin and said, 'Yes, but I'm waiting for Pa to finish with the teeth.' "

By making yourself a character in the joke and

by changing the location from an anonymous restaurant to your bar, you make this joke more believ-
able and more fun for your listeners.

How Not to Tell a Joke

"Have you heard the one about . . . ?"
As a bartender you probably hear more jokes
than anyone. Be a good sport, let your friends know
how you appreciate their humor even if you've
heard the same joke many times before.
It is a mistake to tell a different version of a joke
your guest just told. It's not uncommon to have a
bartender say, "The way I heard that joke was . . ."
While it may be true that you can get a laugh by
telling the joke the "right" way, why risk alien-
ating your guest? This advice isn't a technique, but
a commonsense tip that could very well increase
your tips.

Last but Not Least

Do your friends tell you that you are the funniest
bartender they know? If you have guests laughing
out loud and you don't follow any of our suggestions—that's great! The ultimate rule of joke telling is . . . there are no rules. If it works for you, it
works. Humor is very personal. If you have found
a method of using humor that breaks all the rules
but keeps your friends in stitches, don't change a
thing.

Restocking Your Well of Jokes

People expect bartenders to have a never-ending supply of jokes and stories. Where do you get them? Buying this book is a good start and a wise decision on your part. But a joke book, no matter how good, will only have a limited number of jokes you can tell.

Nothing will provide you with a better source of humorous material than your guests and friends. When you hear a joke that you find funny, ask if it's all right if you can add the joke to your collection. People consider bartenders to be professional humorists; they will be flattered and will probably respond in a positive manner.

Occasionally, someone may not feel comfortable letting you tell one of their best jokes. In that case, just pass; there will always be more stories and jokes making the rounds.

Bartenders are not the only professionals who are noted for their sense of humor. Trading jokes with your stockbroker and swapping stories with your hairstylist are simple ways to increase your stockpile of jokes. You hear jokes all day long. Hop in a cab and the taxi driver tells you a lawyer joke. Buy a bottle of scotch and the salesman repeats the latest political joke.

Collecting new stories and jokes can be as easy as waking up. While you are brushing your teeth listen to the radio and make a mental note of the wisecracks and jokes the disc jockey tells. If it sounds funny to you, it will probably sound funny to your friends.

Keep a notepad handy when you are watching

television. There are lots of great jokes waiting to be borrowed from talk-show hosts delivering their nightly monologue.

You don't have to go too far out of your way to find fresh humorous material. Keep your ears open and soon your guests will think you're the funniest bartender in town.

How to Remember a Joke

"I love jokes, I just can't remember them!"
                    —An Anonymous Bartender

Who hasn't known the bartender who can rattle off one hilarious joke after another? Maybe he's a born comedian or perhaps he's taken a memory course. What is the secret to remembering jokes? The secret is . . . there is no secret! With a little patience and some practice, one can learn how to memorize jokes and stories. Three simple memory techniques are offered to help you remember how to be the life of the party.

The Joke Recipe Technique

As a bartender you are expected to know how to make hundreds of cocktails. The ingredients for the most commonly ordered drinks are easy to remember. Just as you know how to make a margarita by recalling the key ingredients—the tequila, Triple Sec, and lime juice—you can call to mind a funny story by making a note about the joke's key elements—the opening, middle, and punch line. Here's an example of a joke to illustrate the point.

"An old couple went to a crowded hotel and asked for a room. The clerk told them the place was filled up except for the honeymoon suite, but he could put them in there. The husband said, 'The honeymoon suite? We've been married forty years!' The clerk answered, 'Look, if I send you to the main ballroom, it doesn't mean you have to dance.' "

The important words to jot down that will help you remember the opening of the joke are *old couple*. Next, the essence of the joke is the idea of the elderly couple spending the night in the honeymoon suite of an overbooked hotel. Write down *honeymoon suite* to jar your memory. And last, the punch line, "if I send you to the main ballroom, it doesn't mean you have to dance." You will probably remember the entire punch line with the two words *ballroom* and *dance*. In your notebook the entry will read "old couple—honeymoon suite—ballroom, dance." You now have a "recipe" for a joke that is easy to recall.

By using the recipe method for remembering jokes, you can develop your own personal book of humor to have at your fingertips when tending bar. The "book" consists of a few key words from your funny stories and jokes jotted down in a small notebook. In no time you will have a collection of jokes to keep in your hip pocket.

Last Things First

This method—Last Things First—is an easy memory technique used by many professional comedians. Thumb through this book and find a joke that you find funny. It may be less intimidating if you start off with a joke that is short and snappy like this one. . . .

"A couple of goats are having dinner at the city dump. One of the goats finds a roll of film and starts to eat it. He's chewing away and the other goat says to him, 'How's the film?' The first goat says, 'To tell you the truth, I preferred the book.' "

Read the joke over, taking special note of the punch line—the key words at the end—"To tell you the truth, I preferred the book." Repeat the punch line to yourself until you have it memorized. Many people find that if they know the punch line of the joke word for word, the rest of the joke comes to mind easily. You may discover this is true for you, too. Since the punch line is the part of the joke that gets the laugh, make it a habit to memorize these key words exactly as they are written.

Record the Joke

A Martian lands his spaceship in Brooklyn . . . or was it Manhattan . . . or maybe it was in New Jersey? Have you ever heard a funny joke and the next day you just can't seem to remember it? One bartender I know has a simple solution to this frustrating problem. He keeps a small tape recorder behind the bar while he is working. If he hears a funny joke, he may ask the guest to tell the story so he can record it, or he repeats the joke into the tape recorder himself. Either way, the joke is recorded for him to listen to in his free time. Playing the joke over and over is a painless way to learn it.

Listening to your own voice telling a joke can be a powerful memory aid. Once you think you know the joke, record it again, then play it back to make sure you have it down pat.

1

TWO GORILLAS WALK INTO A BAR

Actually, sightings of gorillas in taverns have been rare. However, they do have their fair share of foxes and wolves and an occasional rat. In bars, stories and jokes about animals abound. Here are some of our favorites.

Two gorillas walk into a bar; one of the big apes orders a couple of beers.

The amazed bartender sets the drafts on the bar and says, "That'll be twenty dollars."

The other gorilla pulls out his wallet and pays the tab. The curious bartender leans over and says, "Don't take this the wrong way, but we don't get many gorillas in here."

The first gorilla puts down his drink and responds, "At these prices I'm not surprised!"

A stranger orders a dry martini at Smitty's Bar. He takes a couple of sips and says, "This is the best martini I've ever had; it has just the right amount of vermouth and it's chilled to perfection. I must give you something for being such a great bartender." With that, he reaches into his pocket and hands the bartender a live lobster.

"Thanks," says Smitty, "I guess I can take it home for dinner."

"No, no," says the customer. "He's already had dinner. Take him to a movie."

A guy wanders into a bar carrying a pig that has a wooden leg. The bartender says, "Hey, you can't bring that pig in here! And by the way, why does he have a wooden leg?"

The guy says, "This pig is special. One day he was rooting around the back of my shack when he struck oil. I tore down the shack and built a big fancy house with a swimming pool."

The bartender says, "Yeah, but why does he have a wooden leg?"

"He's a special pig. My son fell into the swimming pool and almost drowned, but the pig jumped in and pulled him out and gave him mouth-to-mouth resuscitation."

The bartender says, "Yeah, but why does he have a wooden leg?"

"This is a special pig. He saved my family's lives. One night a fire broke out in the kitchen; the pig hit the fire alarm, woke us up, and put the fire out before it did any damage."

The bartender says, "Yeah, but why does he have a wooden leg?"

The guy looks at the bartender and says, "A pig like that you don't eat all at once."

A monkey is having a draft in his local tavern. When he's down to the last sip, he spits the beer at the bartender. The monkey apologizes to the bartender: "Please forgive me, you probably think we do this in the jungle all the time. Actually, it's a nervous habit; I just can't seem to break it. It is so embarrassing."

"You'd better see a psychiatrist," says the bartender.

A few weeks later, the monkey comes in the bar again. He sits down and orders a beer. Just as he's about to take the last sip he spits at the bartender.

"Hey, I thought you were going to see a psychiatrist!"

"I have been," said the monkey.

"Well, it's not doing any good."

"Yes, it is," said the monkey, "now I'm not embarrassed about it."

An ad appears in *The New York Times* advertising for a manager to work in a bar near the United Nations. The qualifications are: knowledge of accounting, computer literacy, ten years' experience working in the bar business, and the ability to speak more than one language.

The first applicant for the job is a fox terrier. The dog has his MBA degree in accounting, has taught computer sciences at MIT for the past five years, and ran his own bar in New Jersey for twelve years.

The bar owner is very impressed with the terrier's qualifications, turns to him, and says, "I just have one question. What about the language qualification?"

The dog says, "Meow!"

In the heart of New York's theater district, a guy walks into a bar with a gorilla on a chain. He sits down at the bar and strikes up a conversation with the man sitting next to him. As luck would have it, the man is a talent agent.

The guy introduces the agent to the gorilla.

"This is George, the most talented gorilla on earth. Hit it, George!"

George puts on a tuxedo and takes out a top hat and cane and does an incredible imitation of Fred Astaire, tap-dancing around the bar.

The guy yells out, "Stevie Wonder."

With that, the gorilla puts on a pair of sunglasses, sits down at the piano, and sings all of Stevie Wonder's hit songs.

Then the guys says, "Jay Leno."

The gorilla puts on a suit and necktie, stands up, and begins telling jokes, one funnier than the other, in a perfect imitation of Jay Leno.

Next, the guy calls out, "Shakespeare!"

The gorilla puts on a long velvet cape and does an impression of Laurence Olivier in *Hamlet* and Richard Burton in *Taming of the Shrew*.

"Well," asks the guy, "what do you think of George?"

The agent takes the gorilla aside and says, "I've been in this business for fifty years; I've seen acts come and go. Let me give you some advice . . . just be yourself."

Bill takes a tiny mouse from his coat pocket; he puts the rodent on the bar and orders a beer for himself and a thimbleful for the mouse.

After drinking the beer, the mouse stands on his hind legs and sings a medley of the songs from *The Phantom of the Opera*. The bartender is amazed. He's never seen anything like this.

The man says, "Look, buy us a round of drinks and you can keep the mouse."

The bartender serves them the drinks and says, "I can't believe this, you are giving away a gold mine for a couple of beers."

Bill says, "Hell, all he knows is *Phantom of the Opera*.

Two gorillas walk into a bar. On the television set they're watching the movie *King Kong*. The two gorillas watch for a while, then one turns to the other and says, "That ape is a terrible actor. His movements are stiff as a robot's, and his fur looks like an old rug."

The other gorilla says, "You idiot. That ape isn't real, he's a mechanical fake."

"Gee," says the first gorilla, "you could never tell."

Frank and Mike take a trip to Africa. They are sitting in a bar in Kenya making a bet as to which one of them will be the first to shoot a lion on the safari. Before long the friendly bet develops into a heated argument. Frank bets Mike a hundred dollars that he will be the first. Frank jumps up from his bar stool and says, "I'm going out there right now!" He grabs his rifle and storms out of the bar and heads for the jungle.

An hour later, a lion walks into the bar and roars, "Anyone here know a guy named Frank?"

"I do," a trembling Mike replies.

The lion says, "Well, he owes you a hundred bucks."

Dusty and Clem are drinking red-eye in the Old West Saloon when a herd of cattle stampedes down the road.

"Wow," says Dusty, "I wonder how many there were."

"Three hundred and twenty-seven," says Clem.

"How could you count them?"

"I used a trick my grandpappy taught me—I counted their legs then divided them by four."

A termite crawls into a tavern and says, "Excuse me, is the bar tender in here?"

Three vampire bats fly into a bar. The first bat orders a blood. "Ditto," says the second bat. The third bat asks the bartender for a plasma.

"Let me be sure I've got this right," says the bartender. "That will be a blood, a blood, and a blood lite."

Tom and Mike are sitting in Smitty's Bar and Tom says, "You know I bought a parakeet a few months ago and he doesn't say a word."

Mike says, "Well, when you bought the bird, what else did you get for it?"

Tom said, "I got a cage and bird feed."

"That's your problem," says Mike. "It's a well-known fact that a parakeet won't say a word unless he has something in the cage to make him happy."

"What should I get?" asks Tom.

"Why not buy one of those little plastic ladders. Birds love those things. Your parakeet can hop up and down on the ladder, and it will have so much fun, before you know it, the bird will be talking up a blue streak."

Two weeks later, Tom and Mike meet in the bar. Tom says, "Hey, buddy, great advice! I got the ladder for my parakeet, and this morning I woke up and the parakeet was dead on the bottom of the cage."

Mike is astonished. "You mean to say the poor little thing never said a word before it died?"

Tom says, "Well, now that you mention it, it

might have said something. Just before I found it dead, I heard a small voice say, 'Who moved the ladder?' "

A guy is having a drink and he notices a poker game is going on at one of the tables near the bar. Three guys are playing five-card stud with a French poodle. He walks over to the game and is astonished as he watches the dog win three hands in a row. Finally, he says to one of the guys playing cards with the dog, "I can't believe my eyes; I have never seen such a smart dog in my life."

The guy says, "He's not that smart; whenever he gets a good hand, he wags his tail."

Two elephants are sitting in a bar and one turns to the other and says, "I don't care what they say, I can't remember a thing."

A lion is drinking a gin and tonic in the Safari Lounge when a monkey walks in. The lion strolls over to the ape and growls his most ferocious growl: "Who is the king of the jungle?"

The monkey trembles and says, "You are, lion."

A little time passes and a gnu strolls in; again the lion growls, "Who is the king of the jungle?"

The gnu bows and says, "You are, lion!"

With each new animal that comes into the bar, the scene is replayed. Finally, a Clydesdale wanders into the bar and orders a beer. The lion taps him on the hoof and roars, "Who is the king of the jungle?"

The Clydesdale puts down his beer and picks the lion up by the mane; he tosses him down on the barroom floor, then he stomps on his head with his hooves. The horse takes the lion in his teeth and tosses him outside into the gutter. The lion, battered and bruised, limps back into the bar. He takes his place on a stool, leans over to the bartender, and says, "He didn't have to get mad just because he didn't know the right answer."

The bartender says to a sheep sitting at the bar, "What can I get you?"

The sheep looks up and says, "Moo."

The bartender says, "Sheep don't say, 'moo,' sheep say 'bah.' "

"Shows what you know," says the sheep. "I'm bilingual."

Two Arabian stallions are having a drink in a bar near the city zoo. One horse is telling the other horse about the zoo's newly arrived female zebra. "She's not only beautiful, but she's got a sex drive that won't quit." The other stallion wastes no time and trots over to visit the zebra at the zoo.

A few hours later, he comes back to the bar. His hooves are all scratched, his tail is missing, he's got a black eye, and his lip is cut. "Well, isn't that zebra something?"

The black-and-blue stallion says, "I'm not sure. I couldn't get her pajamas off."

A couple of chickens are having a drink in the Barnyard Bar. The first chicken says, "How's business?"

"Not bad," the other chicken says. "I'm getting $1.10 a dozen for my eggs."

"Really," says the first chicken, "I get a dollar a dozen."

"I get more because my eggs are so much bigger," brags the other chicken.

"Well," says the first chicken, "I'm not going to bust my gut for a lousy ten cents a dozen."

Smitty's elderly aunt gives him a pair of parrots for a Christmas gift. Hoping it would be a good influence on Smitty, the little old lady teaches the parrots to pray. After months of training, the parrots can say grace before meals. And they recite their evening prayers before they are covered for the night.

Smitty likes the birds and keeps them behind the bar in a cage. After a few months, he goes to the pet store and buys a female parrot. He brings the female parrot home and puts her into the cage with the other two.

As he shuts the cage door one parrot turns to the other and says, "It looks like our prayers have been answered."

Bob is opening his bar one day and is amazed to see a gorilla sitting in the oak tree in front of his establishment. He carefully walks into his bar and wastes no time looking up "Gorilla Removal" in the Yellow Pages. He calls the service, and in nothing flat a truck pulls up with the words JOE'S GORILLA REMOVAL written on the side.

A man gets out of the truck carrying a loaded pistol and he has a fierce-looking German shepherd on a leash. "Now, here's the plan," Joe tells Bob. "You hold the gun and I'll climb up the tree and shake the big ape out. When the gorilla falls to the ground, the German shepherd will attack him and go for his private parts. After that, I just throw him in the back of my truck. Any questions?"

"Just one," says Bob. "What's the gun for?"

"If I fall out of the tree, shoot the dog!"

Smitty has a passion for fixing things. He isn't happy unless he has a screwdriver in his hand and is tinkering with something that needs repair in his bar. Unfortunately, his enthusiasm is greater than his skill as a repairman.

One day the cuckoo clock in the bar stops working. "Don't worry," Smitty announces to the customers, "I'll have it fixed in no time." He takes the broken clock into his office, and in a matter of minutes, the top of his desk is littered with gears and springs. After hours and hours of work, Smitty throws the door to his office open and declares in a loud voice, "I've fixed it!" He hangs the clock in its usual place and the customers in the bar wait for the time to sound.

At ten minutes after eight, the cuckoo comes out of his door upside door, hanging by his wing on a spring, and says, "Does anyone know what the hell time it is?"

Bubba is bragging to the bartender, "My dog Butch is the toughest dog ever born. He once took on four pit bulls and they didn't put a scratch on him. There's not a dog alive that can touch my Butch."

Meanwhile, a meek-looking man comes into the bar, taps Bubba on the shoulder, and says, "Excuse me, sir, but I think I owe you an apology. My dog just killed your Butch."

Bubba goes crazy. "That's impossible, how could your dog kill my Butch? What kind of dog is it?"

"A chihuahua," answers the timid man.

"You're putting me on," says Bubba. "How could a tiny chihuahua kill Butch?"

"He got stuck in his throat."

One of the bar's regular customers, Frank, is laid up for six months with two broken legs. He is soon bored with reading and can't stand to watch any more television. One day he notices a tiny little ant crawling on the windowsill. He watches as the small creature makes its way up onto his bed. Frank is impressed with the ant's ability and takes a matchstick and teaches the ant to jump over it. He is delighted with his newfound pet, and soon he is teaching the ant to perform somersaults. Each day he spends all his time training the ant. At the end of two months, the ant can walk on a tiny high wire and ride on the back of a cockroach. The months pass and Frank is still recovering from his accident and is teaching the ant even more amazing tricks.

Finally, Frank is able to walk again. He can't wait to bring his multitalented ant to the bar and show him off. He walks into Smitty's Bar and puts the tiny ant on the counter. He turns to the bartender and says, "See this ant?"

"Oh, sorry," says the bartender as his hand comes down with a *splat*!

Alex walks into a bar with a large baboon. Alex says, "Mind if he mixes my drink?"

"Sure, why not," says the bartender.

The big ape walks behind the bar and puts on an apron and bow tie. He grabs the bottle of gin and precisely pours an ounce and a half into the mixing glass. Then he takes the dry vermouth and adds just a few drops into the glass. The ape stirs the drink, taking care not to bruise the gin. He carefully drains the perfectly made martini into a pre-chilled glass. He finishes the drink off with a lemon twist, rubbing it around the edge of the glass. With a flourish, he places the drink in front of Alex. The baboon takes Alex's money, rings up the cost of the drink in the register, and puts the change in front of him.

"He knows just how I like it," says Alex, taking a sip.

"Wow," says the bartender, "I could make a fortune with that baboon. How much do you want for him?"

"You don't want him; he always forgets to take out for taxes."

A man strolls into a bar with his Great Dane. The man orders himself a drink and asks if it's okay if his dog plays the saloon's piano. The bartender agrees. The dog sits down at the piano and starts playing a medley of show tunes. Before long, he's taking requests from the customers.

The bartender can't believe it. "I never seen anything like your dog. What a talent!"

"Yeah," says the man, "can you believe it, he wants to be a doctor."

John is sipping a beer in Smitty's Tavern when a kangaroo puts down his empty glass, walks over to the wall, and hops up its surface and onto the ceiling. He crosses the ceiling upside down until he reaches the wall where the door is located. He walks down to the top of the doorway, does a somersault to the floor, lands on his tail, and hops out the door.

John regains his composure and says to the bartender, "That's certainly a hell of a way to leave."

"You get used to it," says the bartender with a shrug. "He always leaves without tipping."

A guy walks into a bar with a pig under his arm. "Where did you get that thing?" asks the bartender.

"I won him in a raffle," says the pig.

An avid baseball fan is at home watching the Yankees on TV. Just before the game starts, the crowd sings a rousing rendition of the National Anthem. The man's parrot breaks into song and sings "The Star-Spangled Banner" flawlessly. The man is amazed. Each time a baseball game is on, the parrot sings the National Anthem. The guy sees an opportunity to make some money. That night at his neighborhood bar, he is bragging that his parrot can sing the National Anthem.

The other patrons are not impressed and tell the guy to put his money where his mouth is.

He eagerly takes all their bets and agrees to bring his parrot in for the next game.

The next day the parrot is on display at the bar. The game is just about to begin and all the bettors are gathered around the bird. The baseball crowd is singing the National Anthem and all eyes are on the bird. Nothing happens.

The crowd bursts into laughter and demands their money.

Furious, the man takes the bird home and sets the cage on the kitchen table. He begins sharpening his knife. "That's it for you, I'm totally humiliated, not to mention broke. Now you're going to pay."

"Wait," says the bird, "think of the odds we'll get during the World Series."

An elephant comes into a bar with a large bandage over his left ear.

"What happened to you?" says the bartender.

"I bit myself on the ear," says the elephant.

"That's impossible! How could you bite yourself on the ear?"

"I stood on a chair."

A frisky monkey is having a drink in the Safari Lounge. He looks around, hoping to see a girl monkey to fool around with. There's not one female monkey in the place. It is getting later and later and he's feeling more and more frustrated. Then a lioness walks into the bar. He takes her by surprise, jumps on her, and makes love to her.

When he finishes, he runs out of the lounge and the lioness begins to chase him through the jungle. The monkey comes to a clearing; there's a park bench with a newspaper lying on it. The monkey grabs the paper and begins reading it.

The lioness comes running by and shouts, "Did you see a monkey go by here?"

"The one that screwed the lion?"

"My God," says the lioness. "You mean it's in the paper already?"

Two turtles stop in their local tavern for a beer after work. They have just been served their drinks when it begins to rain. The big turtle says to the little turtle, "Go home and get the umbrella."

The little turtle says, "Yeah, but when I leave, you're going to drink my beer."

"No, I won't," says the big turtle.

"Promise," says the little turtle.

"I promise. Now go get the umbrella."

Time passes and two years later the big turtle says, "I guess he's not coming back. I'm going to drink his beer."

As he reaches for the glass a small voice calls

from outside the door, "If you touch that beer, I won't go home and get the umbrella."

Every Sunday evening a little old lady stops by Smitty's for a glass of sherry; she always has her pet monkeys, Mildred and Mortimer, with her. One day the old lady comes in and tells Smitty that after a long and happy life, Mortimer died, and a few days later Mildred died of a broken heart.

"I'm going to taking Mildred and Mortimer to the taxidermist," she tells Smitty.

"Do you want them mounted?" Smitty asks.

"Oh, no," she says, "just holding hands."

A guy walks into a bar with a duck under his arm. The bartender says, "What are you doing with that ugly pig?"

"This isn't a pig, it's a duck."

"I was talking to the duck."

A tough-looking guy swaggers into a pub in the remote outback of Australia with a crocodile on a string. The bar clears out when the customers spot the huge reptile.

"Do you serve Americans?" growls the man.

"We serve anyone," answers the bartender.

"Good," says the man. "I'll have a beer, and an American for my crocodile."

Every St. Patrick's Day, the owner of Duffy's Tavern celebrates by asking his cook to make corned beef and cabbage for the customers.

The cook comes out of the kitchen and says, "I'm not so sure I like the way this corned beef looks. It may be bad."

It's too late to order any more beef, so the owner

suggests they feed it to his pet dog, Jeeves. Jeeves eats the corned beef and begs for more. They decide to serve the corned beef. The tavern is packed and just about everyone is eating the corned beef and cabbage. The cook walks into the bar and whispers to the owner, "Jeeves is dead."

The owner tries to act calm; he goes into the office and calls the hospital and tells them to expect a rash of patients. He is wondering just what the first symptoms will be. He goes into the kitchen and says to the cook, "Where is Jeeves? I want to see him."

"He's lying in the gutter," says the cook, "right where the car ran over him."

A couple of frogs are sitting in a bar. A fly buzzes by and one frog catches it with his tongue. The other frog turns to him and says, "Time sure is fun when you're having flies."

A guy walks into a bar in a college town with a mule, the team's mascot.

"Get that jackass out of here," yells the bartender.

"He's not a jackass, he's a mule!"

"I'm talking to the mule."

"Sorry," says the bartender to a guy with a St. Bernard. "We don't allow dogs in here."

"This is Rex the talking dog."

"Yeah, I've heard that one before," says the bartender.

"I'll show you." The man turns to the dog and says, "Rex, what's on top of the house?"

"Roof," says the dog.

"Get out," says the bartender.

"Wait," says the man, turning to the dog. "Rex, what does sandpaper feel like?"

"Ruff!"

"You and your dog get out!" says the bartender.

"One more try," says the man. "Rex, who was the greatest New York Yankee of all time?"

"Ruth!" says the dog.

"That does it," the bartender says, and jumps over the bar and tosses the man and the dog into the street.

The dog looks at the man and says, "Do you think I should have said DiMaggio?"

Tom Cat is sitting at the bar when in walks Miss Kitty with ten little kittens trailing her. Tom Cat says to her, "Hiya, honey!"

"Don't you honey me. You told me we were only wrestling."

Jake goes into a pet shop looking for a bird to keep him company while he tends bar. He sees a parrot that he likes, but the bird only has one wing. The pet-store owner notices that the man is considering buying the bird and says, "I'll tell you what, since the bird only has one wing, I'll sell it to you for twenty bucks."

"Well, doesn't the fact that he only has one wing throw him off balance?"

"You'd think so," says the pet-store owner, "but he's learned to use his beak as a crutch."

Jake buys the parrot and takes him to work. He and the bird get along fine. He even lets the bird out of the cage to sit on his shoulder while he's pouring drinks. To get on his shoulder the bird has to peck on the guy's arm with its sharp beak.

The bartender calls the pet store to get some advice. "It's easy," says the guy at the pet store. "All you have to do is file down his beak, but be careful not to file it down too much or the bird won't be able to eat and he'll starve to death!"

A few weeks later, Jake shows up in the pet store. "How's your parrot?" asks the owner.

"Dead," says Jake.

"I told you not to file down his beak too much!"

"That wasn't the problem," Jake says. "He was dead when I took his head out of the vise."

A blind man and his guide dog stroll into a bar. He picks the dog up by the tail and swings the animal over his head. The bartender says, "Can I get you anything?"

"No thanks," says the blind man. "I'm just looking around."

A deer, a skunk, and a duck wander into a cocktail lounge. They order drinks and the bartender says, "That'll be eight dollars."

The deer says, "I don't have a buck."

The skunk says, "And I don't have a scent."

"Go ahead," says the duck, "put it on my bill."

Two gorillas walk into a bar and they each order a shot of tequila. They drink the tequila down, put a ten-dollar bill on the bar, and walk out without saying a word.

The bartender picks up the bill, puts it in his pocket, and says, "Those damn gorillas! They come in here, give me a ten-dollar tip, and then they leave without paying."

A grizzly bear wanders into a tavern, sits down at the bar, and orders a drink. A guy walks up behind the grizzly and wraps his arms around the beast and gives him a big hug. The bear goes wild and takes the guy and slams him down on the barroom floor and grinds his paw into the man's face. Then the giant bear stands up on his hind legs, grabs the guy by his hair, and throws him out the door.

The man, black and blue, stumbles back into the bar, crawls up to the bar, and says to the bartender, "Give some women a fur coat and they think they own the world."

A hawk, a mountain lion, and a skunk are having a drink in the Wilderness Bar. They get into a discussion as to which one of them is the most powerful.

"It's me," says the hawk, "I can swoop down and attack my prey before they even know I'm there."

"And I," says the lion, "have the most powerful claws and teeth in all of nature."

"But I," says the skunk, "with just a small flick of my tail can drive off both of you."

Just then a grizzly bear walks into the bar and settles the argument by eating all of them . . . hawk, lion, and stinker.

Stan tells the bartender that his dog can count. The bartender just shakes his head and walks away.

"No," says Stan, "I can prove it. Rex, how many bartenders are here?" The dog stands up on his hind legs, looks behind the bar, gets down, and makes one circle around the man.

"One. See, he can count," says Stan.

"That doesn't prove anything," says the bartender.

"Okay. Rex, how many bar stools are in here?" Rex goes down the bar and touches each stool with his nose, then he makes ten circles around Stan.

"It's just a trick," says the bartender.

"No, he can really count. Rex, how many bottles of whiskey are behind the bar?"

Rex jumps up on the bar, spends a few minutes looking at the bottles, then he jumps down and starts humping Stan's leg, then he picks up a mixing spoon with his teeth and waves it back and forth.

"What's that supposed to mean?" asks the bartender.

"Rex just said you have more frigging whiskey bottles than you can shake a stick at."

A camel strides into a bar with an Egyptian mummy riding on its back. The camel kneels down and the mummy crawls off and makes his way to the bar.

"What will you have?" asks the bartender.

"Nothing for me," says the mummy. "I just came in here to unwind."

A parrot, a parakeet, and a mynah bird fly into a bar. First the parrot orders. "Bartender, I'd like a cold beer, please."

"And I'd like a gin and tonic," says the parakeet.

"Give me a scotch on the rocks," says the mynah bird.

"Sorry," says the bartender. "I'll give you the beer, the gin and tonic, but not the scotch."

"Why not?" ask the birds.

"Because," answers the bartender, "we don't serve mynahs."

The guys at Smitty's Bar are looking out the window and they see a circus parade going down the street. There are clowns, marching bands, and floats. At the end of the parade is a line of elephants all holding on to each other's tail. Just as the last elephant is walking by, a man drives through the intersection in his pickup truck and hits the elephant.

The next day the guy is sitting in Smitty's having a drink. He tells Smitty that he got a bill from the circus for hitting the elephant. "Can you believe it?" says the guy. "I was billed for two million dollars."

"Two million?" says Smitty. "That's a lot for hitting one elephant."

"Yeah," says the guy, "but the chain reaction pulled the tails out of all the others."

A monkey is sitting on the window ledge in a bar playing a harmonica. The ape is so engrossed in his music he doesn't realize that his tail is in a pitcher of beer on the table. A guy walks up to the bartender and complains that the monkey has his tail in his beer.

"Don't tell me," says the bartender, "tell the monkey."

"Hey," says the man to the monkey, "do you know your tail is in my beer?"

"I'm not sure," says the monkey. "Hum a few bars and I'll fake it."

"Hey, bartender, why did the turtle cross the road?"

"Beats me."

"Because it was the chicken's day off."

Bob walks into a bar with two gorillas. One of the gorillas sits down at the piano and the other one takes out a violin. They play a selection of classical music and then take requests from the customers in the booths. The bartender says to Bob, "I can't believe this, how did they learn to play?"

"Well," says Bob, "the gorilla on the violin took the lessons and the gorilla on the piano plays by ear."

A mongrel dog is sipping a drink at the bar when a French poodle comes in and sits down next to him. They strike up a conversation and the poodle says to the mongrel, "What kind of dog are you?"

"I'm a police dog," whispers the mongrel.

"Funny, you don't look like a police dog," says the poodle.

"Shh . . . I'm working undercover."

A guy comes running into a tavern in the woods in Wisconsin. "I just shot an elk," he yells.

"Never saw any elk around here," says the bartender. "Are you sure it was an elk?"

"Positive," says the man. "I saw the membership card in his wallet."

In the backwoods of Minnesota, a guy is having a drink at the local tavern. He notices a giant moose head hung on the brick wall over the bar. The bartender explains that usually moose aren't seen in this part of the country, but during mating season, a moose has been known to wander into town.

"My gosh," says the customer, "and he ran right through that thick brick wall."

The neighborhood bar has a sign-up sheet posted on the back wall for their softball team. A turkey trots into the bar, takes a look at the sheet and puts his name down.

It's the first day of practice and the turkey grabs a glove and trots out to center field. The turkey is a great fielder and catches everything that comes his way. The manager is very impressed with the way the bird is playing and he says, "Hey, turkey, you're great! I was talking to the other guys and we'd like you to play on our team."

"On one condition," says the turkey.

"What's that?" asks the manager.

"We play through November."

A guy walks into Smitty's Bar; he reaches into his pocket and tosses dust all over the counter.

"What the hell are you doing?" yells the bartender.

"I'm spreading my magic dust to keep the tigers away," says the guy.

"There isn't a tiger within ten thousand miles of here."

"See, it works!"

A guy is having a drink in a bar and he finds a bug in his drink. Outraged, he storms out of the bar, and when he gets home he writes an angry letter to the bar owner. A week later he gets a letter from the bar. It says, "Dear Sir: Your letter was a great cause of concern to us. We have never received a complaint like yours in all the fifteen years we have been in business. We will do everything possible to make sure that nothing like this ever happens again." The guy is satisfied until he sees a note fall out of the envelope. The note says, "Send this guy the bug letter."

Smitty hires a new bartender and he is working his first shift behind the bar. Things are going fine and then the new guy says, "Smitty, do limes have feathers?"

"What are you talking about? Of course not!" says Smitty.

"Oh, hell," says the bartender, "I just squeezed your parakeet into a vodka and tonic."

A grasshopper is sitting on top of the bar. The bartender notices him and says, "You know something, buddy, they named a drink after you."

"No kidding," says the grasshopper, "they've got a drink named Bruce?"

Chris and his pet dog walk into a sports bar in Chicago. Everyone in the bar is watching the Northwestern football game on the bar's television. No one is watching more intently than Chris's dog.

It's the third quarter and Northwestern makes a touchdown. The crowd in the bar goes crazy and the dog starts to howl and run around in circles. He pulls down the Northwestern pennant from behind the bar and holds it in his mouth, waving it around.

"What's with your dog?" asks the bartender.

"He's a diehard Northwestern fan and he goes crazy every time Northwestern scores a touchdown."

"What does he do when Northwestern wins a game?"

"I don't know," says Chris, "I've only had him six years."

An earthworm is crawling across Smitty's bar and right there next to him is the most beautiful earthworm he has ever seen.

"Baby," the worm says, "where have you been all my life?"

"You jerk! I'm your other end."

A chicken and a pig are having a drink together in the Barnyard Tavern. The chicken says, "Let's go in business together. We could open a ham-and-eggs restaurant. It's perfect for us."

The pig says, "You're a chicken; for you it's a day's work. But for me it's a real sacrifice."

A guy walks into a bar with a lioness by his side.

"You can't bring that lion in here," says the bartender.

"I know it's a little unusual," says the man, "but I am a research scientist, and we're looking for volunteers who might be willing to have sex with this sex-starved lioness. It's worth a thousand dollars if anyone is interested."

"I would be," says a guy sitting at the bar.

"Great," says the scientist, "let's go back to the clinic."

"Just one thing," says the man. "Look, I'm a little pressed for cash, can I pay you fifty bucks a month?"

A sparrow is waiting for his buddy the pigeon in a local bar. Finally, his friend the pigeon shows up. The pigeon's feathers are sticking out every which way and he's all shaken up.

"What happened to you?" asks the sparrow.

"It was the craziest thing. I was on my way over here to meet you and I flew down very low over the park to see what was going on. Before I knew what was happening, I got caught in a badminton game."

A guy wants to do something special for his parrot's birthday and he decides to take the bird out to his local pub to celebrate. They walk into the bar and settle themselves into a table near the bar. Everyone in the bar is staring at the strange couple.

Finally, the parrot turns around and says, "What are you looking at? I'm over twenty-one."

"It was terrible," says the bartender to the cop. "Just as I was closing up, two elephants came in here and held me up."

"What did they look like?" asks the cop.

"They were big and gray . . . you know elephants."

"Well," says the cop, "if they had big ears, they were African elephants, and if they had small ears, they would be from India."

"How the hell should I know what kind of ears they had? They were wearing stocking masks."

A gorilla from the local zoo is sitting at the bar. The ape is reading from the book of Genesis in the Bible and he also has a copy of Darwin's *Origin of Species*.

"What are you reading those for?" asks the bartender.

"I'm trying to figure out," says the gorilla, "if I am my brother's keeper, or if I am my keeper's brother."

A bar is famous for its pair of monkeys, Mable and Mike, that keep the customers entertained with their antics. One night the monkeys are nowhere in sight.

"Hey, what happened to Mable and Mike?" asks a customer.

"It's mating season," says the bartender. "They're out in back doing their thing."

"If I throw out some peanuts, will they come out here?" asks the customer.

"I doubt it," says the bartender. "Would you?"

A guy walks into a bar in Canada; sitting on one of the bar stools is a huge stuffed grizzly bear.

"Where did you get that bear?" asks the guy.

"I shot him when me and my uncle went out hunting last winter," says the bartender.

"What's he stuffed with?" asks the guy.

"My uncle."

A dog is sitting at the piano in the bar playing a Bach fugue. Just as he is about to finish, a customer at the end of the bar starts a loud conversation with his friend. The dog stops his playing and growls at the man.

"Don't worry," says the bartender, "his Bach is worse than his bite."

One of Smitty's customer's gave him a pet parrot to keep him company. The bird is doing fine for the first few months and then he grows listless. Smitty takes the bird to the vet and the doctor tells him that it is mating season and the bird needs a female to perk him up. He buys a beautiful female parrot for $500 and can't wait to see his parrot's reaction when he gets the bird home.

As soon as Smitty puts the female in the cage, his parrot starts tearing out all her feathers with his beak.

"What the hell are you doing?" yells Smitty.

"You paid $500 for her, didn't you?" says the parrot. "For that price, I want her naked."

A caterpillar is crawling across the bar. He looks out the window at a butterfly flying by. The caterpillar looks at the bartender and says, "You'll never get me up in one of those things."

Three dogs—an English terrier, a French poodle, and a Chinese chow—are sitting in a bar in Europe discussing the merits of their countries.

"I love England," says the terrier. "I have lots of meadows to run in and they always serve me rare roast beef just the way I like it."

"In Paris," says the poodle, "I have the best of everything—a beautiful château, beautiful gardens to play in, and I have champagne with my evening meal."

"In China," says the chow, "I am treated like a king. I have the finest food, I live in a palace, and I have my run of the countryside. Still I would like to live in America."

"But why?"

"I like to bark once in a while."

A parakeet flies into a bar and orders a drink. The bartender says to the bird, "Say, I wonder if you could tell me something. Which is smarter, a chicken or a parakeet."

"The parakeet, of course," says the bird.

"What makes you parakeets smarter than chickens?"

"Ever heard of Kentucky Fried Parakeet?"

A guy walks into a bar and a dog is tending bar. "What's the matter," says the dog, "haven't you ever seen a German shepherd tending bar before?"

"It's not that," says the man. "Whatever happened to the French poodle?"

Two lions are having a drink, and one says to the other, "My kids are doing great. One's with an NFL football team and the other one is in the movies."

"Hey, Smitty," says a customer, sitting at the bar, "what kind of bird is that?"

"Oh," says Smitty, "that's a Crunchy Bird."

"I never heard of a Crunchy Bird."

"Just watch," says Smitty. He takes a newspaper off the bar and throws it down on the floor, then he turns to the bird and says, "Crunchy Bird, my paper!" The bird swoops down and attacks the newspaper. He rips it to shreds until there's nothing left but tiny pieces of confetti.

"Wow," says the impressed customer, "can I try?"

"Be my guest," says Smitty.

The customer takes off his shoe and puts it on the bar and says, "Crunchy Bird, my shoe!" The bird flies down off his perch and picks the shoe up in his beak. He slams the shoe down on the bar and starts attacking it. In no time, the shoe is reduced to nothing but a few pieces of leather and a shoelace. Then the bird flies back to his perch behind the bar.

A tough-looking guy walks into Smitty's. He yells, "Gimme a drink." He looks around the bar snarling and says, "What the hell are you looking at?" After a few minutes of uneasy silence, the guy notices the bird and says to Smitty, "What the hell is that?"

"That's a Crunchy Bird," says Smitty.

The tough guy snorts and says, "Crunchy Bird, my ass!"

A sexy-looking camel slinks into the Pyramid Bar in Egypt. She's wearing a tight-fitting dress, a pair of red high heels, and has on too much makeup. She sits down at the bar and lights up a cigarette.

A male camel sits down next to her and says, "Hey, baby, I'd like a little action. How much?"

"That all depends," says the hooker camel.

"On what?" asks the male.

"One hump or two."

Ruffy, the bartender's pet dog, trots into the bar with the Sunday paper in his teeth. He puts the newspaper down on the floor and starts turning the pages with his paws.

"Hey, bartender," says one of the customers, "I didn't know Ruffy could read."

"Don't let him kid you," says the bartender, "he just likes to look at the funny papers."

The customers in the bar are watching *Gone With the Wind* on television. The bartender's dog sits at his master's feet watching the movie intently. The dog growls when the Yankees burn down Tara. He drools when Rhett carries Scarlett up to the bedroom and he cries when Rhett walks out the door in the final scene.

A customer leans over the bar and says, "I can't believe how your dog is reacting to the movie."

"Neither can I," says the bartender. "He hated the book."

"So what do you do for a living?" asks the bartender.

"I work for the circus. I wrestle alligators underwater. And sometimes when the lion tamer takes a day off, I take his place and put my head inside a lion's mouth."

"How do you manage to stay alive?"

"I do a little carpentry on the side."

A guy walks into a bar with King, his Great Dane. He strikes up a conversation with the beautiful woman sitting at the bar. Before long, she agrees to go back to his apartment. They are sitting on the couch having a nightcap and he tells her that his dog does tricks with women and asks her if she would like to see.

"Sure," she said, "I love dogs."

"Take off your clothes and lie on the bed," says the guy.

So the woman goes into the bedroom and takes off all her clothes. The dog is sitting by the side of the bed, just staring at her.

"Well," says the woman, "when does he do his trick?"

"King," says the guy as he takes off his clothes, "I'm only going to show you this trick one more time."

Two gorillas are having a beer in a bar; they look around at all the human customers and the one gorilla says in a hushed voice to the other, "I know it's hard to believe, but look at their hands and their faces, how they walk upright. I'm telling you—we are descended from man."

An elephant and a mouse walk into a bar and the elephant says to the bartender, "I'd like to buy my best buddy in the whole world a drink."

The bartender says, "You don't often see an elephant and a mouse who are friends."

"It happened like this," says the mouse. "One day I was walking in the jungle and I happened to fall into a deep pit. I was screaming for help and the elephant heard me. He squatted down over the pit and I grabbed hold of his giant thing and pulled myself out of the pit."

"And wouldn't you know it," says the elephant, "a few days later I am walking in the jungle and I fall into a pit. I am yelling for help and the mouse hears me. He runs and gets a Porsche and ties a rope around it and lowers it into the pit. I grab hold of the car and pull myself up."

"I get it," says the bartender. "The moral of the story is, if you don't have a big thing, then you better have a Porsche!"

Duffy, the bartender, always brings his pet pit bull, Killer, to work with him. One day a guy walks into the bar with the strangest-looking dog Duffy has ever seen. The dog is long and red and has rough hairless skin. The strange dog crawls up to the bar and takes a bite from one of the bar stools. Killer takes one look at the dog and hides in the back room.

"Say, what kind of dog is that?" asks Duffy.

"Well," said the guy, "before I cut off his tail and painted him red, we called him an alligator."

A gorilla walks into a bar and sits down and asks the bartender for a martini straight up. The gorilla drinks the martini, eats the olive, then he chews the glass and spits out the stem. The gorilla thanks the bartender, pays his check, and leaves.

"I can't believe what I just saw," says one of the customers.

"Neither can I," says Smitty. "The stem's the best part."

A man and a dog sit down together at the bar. The bartender says, "What can I get for you?"

The man gets upset and says, "Does it look like I am alone? Ask the dog if he would like anything."

The dog and the man spend the evening sitting at the bar, drinking and watching the baseball game on TV. As they are getting ready to leave, the bartender looks at the man and says, "That'll be ten dollars." And he hands the man the check.

"Don't you understand anything?" says the man as he throws the check in front of the dog. "I'm his guest."

Some of the guys are getting a foursome together to play in the bar's annual golf tournament. One day a gorilla comes into the bar and asks if he could play on the team. The guys decide to give the ape a chance. They take him out to the driving range to see what he can do.

The gorilla takes a couple of practice swings then he hits the ball 400 yards. Arnold Palmer couldn't have done any better. The other golfers are impressed and agree to let the gorilla play in their foursome.

The day of the tournament arrives and the big ape is ready to play. They get out to the first green and the gorilla tees off. The ball sails through the air 450 yards and lands just inches from the hole. The other three players are beside themselves with joy. The caddie hands the gorilla a putter, the gorilla swings, and hits the ball ... 450 yards.

A dog walks into a bar. He has a stethoscope around his neck and he's carrying a black bag.

"Excuse me," says the bartender, "are you a doctor?"

"Yes, I am," says the dog.

"I never met a dog who went to medical school," says the bartender.

"Let me tell you a little story," says the dog. "When I was a young pup, all I wanted to do was bark, scratch my fleas, chase cars, and play fetch with my master. My father took me aside and handed me a book on medicine and said, 'You can be anything you want.' So I gave up barking and scratching fleas. I even gave up chasing cars and playing fetch. I studied day and night and graduated with top honors from my school. I took my father's advice to heart and that's why I am what I am today."

"The world's best doctor."

"No," says the dog, "the world's worst dog."

A hunter comes running into a bar in northern Minnesota and says to the bartender, "I just ran smack into a bear."

"Did you give him both barrels?"

"Hell, I gave him the whole gun!"

The bartender turns on the cable channel in the bar and everyone begins watching a bullfight being broadcast from Mexico. The bullfighter spreads out his cape and the bull comes within inches of goring him. Over and over again, the bull attacks and the bullfighter spreads his cape, flipping it away at the last second. One of the guys looks up and says, "That bull is never going to run into that sack unless he holds it still."

An elderly couple, Rosie and Mike, own a local tavern. One day they are discussing the fact that one of them may die before the other. "No matter which of us goes first," says Rosie, "the other one will come back to this very bar and tell the other one what it's like in the hereafter."

Mike dies and about a month later just as Rosie is closing up the bar she hears a voice. "Rosie . . . Rosie . . . Rosie, it's me, Mike."

"Mike, is it really you? Tell me, what's it like?"

"It's beautiful here and so relaxing," says Mike.

"Tell me more. How do you spend your day?"

"I just roam about looking at the scenery, then I have a little something to eat."

"What else do you do?"

"Then I take a little nap."

"Anything else?"

"Then I go over and visit the cows. . . ."

"They have cows in heaven?"

"Heaven?" says Mike. "Who said anything about heaven? I'm a bull in Montana."

A dog says to the bartender, "Did I ever tell you about the time I was sitting on my front porch and I chased the mailman down the street. I bit him on the ankle, and he was so upset he quit his job at the post office?"

"Look, Fido," says the bartender, "you've been

coming in here every day for two months and every time you tell me the same story!"

"I know," says the dog. "I just like to talk about it."

Two sharks swim into the Ocean Bar. They order a couple of beers and one shark turns to the other and says, "Who was that lady I saw you with last night?"

"That was no lady," says the other shark, "that was dinner."

Jack, the bar owner, saves up for years to go on an African safari. Finally, he takes the trip and no one hears from him for months. Then one day the bartender gets a fax message telling him that Jack has been killed by a tiger. The next day a large crate is delivered to the bar, the bartender opens it, and inside is a dead tiger.

The bartender sends a fax. "Mistake made. Tiger in coffin, not Jack."

A fax message comes back saying, "No mistake! Tiger in coffin, Jack in tiger."

Two ducks waddle into a bar. They sit on the bar stools and the bartender places a dish of water in front of them. The ducks put their heads in the dish and drink down all the water. They thank the bartender and waddle out.

"Hey, bartender, what was that all about?" asks one of the customers.

"Those ducks are here once a month," says the bartender. "They come in here to liquidate their bills."

A prehistoric-looking animal, no bigger than a dog, crawls into a bar in Scotland. The bartender looks at the strange animal and says, "Excuse me, but what kind of animal are you?"

"I'm the Loch Ness Monster."

"Aren't you kind of small to be the Monster?"

"Well," says the Monster, "you know how the press always exaggerates everything."

An army private runs into a bar near his base and yells, "I just ran over an animal out there on the highway."

"What kind?" asks the bartender.

"I don't know. But it had two stripes."

"Well," says the bartender, "it's either a skunk or a corporal."

A guy walks into a bar with a cat and a dog. The bartender says, "What will you have?"

The dog looks at the bartender and says, "I'll have a beer, the cat would like a gin and tonic, and my master will have a brandy."

"I can't believe it," says the bartender, "your dog can talk."

"Don't let him fool you," says the guy. "The cat's a ventriloquist."

Bill is having a beer when he notices that at one of the tables a dog is playing chess with a man. He can't believe his eyes and he watches them play for a little while. He says to the man, "This is amazing. That is the smartest dog I've ever seen."

"He's not so smart," says the man playing chess, "I've beat him three games out of five."

A kangaroo hops into a tavern in the Australian outback.

"Give me a drink," says the kangaroo, "I had a rough day at work."

"Where do you work?" asks the bartender.

"At the Aussie brewery," says the kangaroo.

"You work at the brewery?"

"Sure," says the kangaroo. "Where did you think they get their hops!"

Two gorillas walk into a bar and the bartender says, "Look, I can put you two up for the night, but you'll have to sleep in the barn with my eighteen-year-old daughter."

One gorilla looks at the other and says, "Just our luck, we're in the wrong joke."

2

HAPPY HOUR

It has been a grueling day. Time for a cold beer, a sympathetic ear, and some good cheer. These jokes will make every hour a happy hour for you.

Smitty is interviewing for a new bartender. He asks the guy applying for a job how he became interested in tending bar.

"Actually," says the guy, "I learned to appreciate the value of mixing drinks when I was a forest ranger. Before I went off into the wilderness on my first assignment, my fellow rangers gave me a farewell party. As a going-away gift, they gave me a martini-making kit, a bottle of gin, vermouth, a mixer, stirrer, and a bottle of olives. I was confused. Why would I need a martini set in the wilds? A more experienced ranger set me straight.

" 'You'll find this could be the most important piece of equipment you have. You may be out there in the wilderness totally alone for weeks, maybe months. Soon you'll remember your martini set. You'll take it out and begin to make yourself a martini, and within thirty seconds there will be someone at your side saying, "That's not the way to make a martini." ' "

Mac is enjoying a cocktail after a hard day at the office. A beautiful young woman sits down next to him, takes a sip of her drink, then turns to him and says, "I'll do anything you want for five hundred dollars."

"Anything?" asks Mac.

"Anything!" she purrs.

"This must be my lucky day," Mac says as he takes the money from his wallet. "Go to 2259 Washington Street and paint my house."

"Hey, bartender, what do you get when you cross an insomniac, an agnostic, and a dyslexic?"

"I don't know."

"Someone who stays up all night trying to figure out if there really is a dog."

A stranger in a pub orders a scotch on the rocks. After a few minutes, he starts an argument with one of the regular customers. The bartender takes the man by the elbow and shows him the door. "Sorry, sir, but I run a respectable establishment. Don't ever come in here again!"

A few minutes later the man wanders in again, walks up to the bar, and orders a drink. The bartender eyes him coldly and says, "You must have a double!"

The man says, "Yeah, make it a scotch."

A couple orders a bottle of the bar's finest French champagne.

"Celebrating something special?" asks the bartender as he uncorks the bottle.

"We've saved enough money to go to Europe," answers the man.

"Wonderful, when do you leave?"

"As soon as we save enough to come back."

Bill is traveling on vacation in England. He opens his wallet and discovers that someone has slipped him a fake fifteen-dollar bill. He thinks that it will be easy to pass it off in a bar. He orders a pint of ale in a nearby pub. He drinks it down and puts the fifteen-dollar bill on the counter. The bartender takes the bill and puts it in his register and gives him his change . . . two seven-dollar bills.

Norman settles himself in at the bar and orders a drink from the waitress. He's reading *The Wall Street Journal* when three tough-looking guys in black leather burst into the bar and begin to harass him. One of the thugs picks up Norman's brandy and drinks it straight down. The other takes the bag of beer nuts from Norman's hand and smashes them under his heel. The third belches in his face. Norman calmly picks up his newspaper and walks out of the bar.

One of the thugs turns to the waitress and says, "He's not much of a man, is he?"

"And he's not much of a driver," she says. "He just backed up his Mercedes and ran over three motorcycles."

An embarrassed patient is in the emergency room of the local hospital. "Nurse, that champagne glass I sat on, how can you be certain the doctor got all the pieces out?"

"Simple," she says. "We will reconstruct the glass."

A man is talking to his lawyer over drinks. "I want to buy a birthday gift for my rich old uncle. The poor old guy can hardly get around, his eyesight is failing, his hands shake, and his legs aren't steady. Have any gift suggestions?"

The lawyer thinks for a moment, then says, "Have you given any thought to a nice can of floor wax?"

A bartender wants to hire a new waitress and he decides to have a psychologist help him decide. The psychologist tests fifty applicants and eliminates all but three. He meets with each of them to administer the final test and the bartender watches. He asks the first one, "How much is three and three?"

She says "Six."

He asks the second and she says, "It could be thirty-three."

And the third woman says, "It could be six or it could be thirty-three."

When they leave the room, the psychologist says, "The first woman gave the logical answer. The second woman gave an answer that showed imagination. And the third woman shows that she is both logical and imaginative. So which one will you hire?"

"That's easy," says the bartender. "The blonde in the short skirt."

Just before closing time at the neighborhood bar, Frank realizes he has lost his wallet. He jumps up on the bar and calls out, "I've lost my wallet with eight hundred dollars in it. Whoever finds it will get a reward of fifty dollars."

A voice from the back room yells, "I'll give seventy-five."

Balancing the books at the end of the month is not one of the bar owner's favorite tasks. He makes a valiant effort one Sunday morning, and after hours and hours of work, he finally manages to come up with a figure that satisfies him. One of his customers is looking over his shoulder at the books: "bar towels—$243.24; cleaning supplies—$587.98; ashtrays—$29.50." Then he reads an entry for "ESP—$1,227.39."

"What does ESP mean?" asks the customer.

"Error some place."

The bar is packed to capacity when an enormously fat woman walks in. She stands for a moment and glares at the seated customers. Then she yells, "Isn't some gentleman going to offer me a seat?"

A little wisp of a man stands up and says, "I am willing to make a contribution."

A widow is brought into Smitty's Bar by a group of mourners after her husband's funeral. She is there not ten minutes when an insurance agent comes in and hands her a check for $500,000. "You know," she sobs, "William was such a good man. Why, I would not hesitate to give fifteen thousand dollars of this to have him back right now."

A stockbroker is complaining to his bartender: "You know I spent forty thousand dollars on my daughter's education and she marries a guy who only makes twenty thousand dollars a year."

"What's the problem?" asks the bartender. "You're still getting a fifty-percent return on your money."

During a recent heat wave, a guy collapses on the sidewalk in front of a tavern. A crowd gathers and begins offering suggestions.

"Give that poor man a drink of whiskey," a little old lady says.

"Give him some air," says one man.

"Get him to a hospital," says someone else.

"Give him some whiskey," says the little old lady.

"Keep his feet elevated," a woman shouts.

"Give him some whiskey," repeats the little old lady.

The suggestions continue until suddenly the victim sits up and yells, "Will you all just shut up and listen to the little old lady!"

A holdup man rushes into the overcrowded bar and shouts, "All you mother———s get outta here."

Everyone runs out of the bar in a hail of bullets ... all except one man, who stands calmly at the bar sipping his drink.

"Well?" says the guy, waving his gun.

"Certainly were a lot of them, weren't there?"

George answers an ad for a bartending position at Smitty's Bar. He's talking to the bartender while waiting to be interviewed. The bartender leans across the bar and says in a low voice, "You seem like a nice guy. I'm going to give you a word of advice. Smitty is a good pal and a terrific boss, but he is very sensitive about the fact that he has no ears. During the interview, he'll ask you if you notice anything odd about him. Whatever you do, don't mention anything about his ears!"

After a short time, George is called into Smitty's office. The interview is going great, and just as the bartender predicted, Smitty asks George if he notices anything odd about him.

George hesitates for a moment, then says, "Yes, I do! You're wearing contact lenses."

"That's amazing," cries Smitty. "The fact that you noticed I am wearing contact lenses shows you have a keen eye for detail. I like that in my employees. Tell me, how can you tell that I'm wearing contacts?"

"Easy," says George. "You'd be wearing glasses if you had any ears."

A bar is located across the street from a school for the hearing impaired. Every evening after classes, members of the faculty come into the bar and have a drink. They use sign language to talk and sometimes their conversations become quite intense.

One afternoon a group of the teachers are sitting at a table and are being overly rambunctious in their sign language: their hands are held high, and they are swaying back and forth.

The bartender becomes quite agitated and says to one of his customers sitting at the bar, "Now they'll never go home."

"What do you mean?" asks the customer.

"You can't get them out of here once they start singing!"

Jack is having a rough time making a go of it in his men's clothing shop. He is sitting in Finnigan's Bar after an especially slow day. Finnigan takes his order and says, "I hear you had a fire at your place last week."

"Shh," says Jack, "that was next week."

An eighty-seven-year-old man is in a bar crying his eyes out. The bartender walks over and says, "What seems to be the problem?"

"I just got back from my honeymoon," says the old man, wiping his eyes. "I married a twenty-five-year-old aerobics instructor. She is the most beautiful woman in the world, the sex is great. I've never been happier in my life."

"So why the tears?" asked the bartender.

"I can't remember where I live."

Ben and Mickey are in the bar watching the six o'clock news. A news story shows a man standing on the Brooklyn Bridge about to jump. Ben pipes up and says to Mickey, "I've got twenty bucks here that says the guy won't jump."

"It's a bet," says Mickey."

The guy is standing there for about twenty seconds when all of a sudden, he takes a leap from the bridge and plummets to his death.

"You win," says Ben, "here's your twenty dollars."

"I can't take your money," says Mickey. "I knew he was going to jump. I saw the news earlier."

"I did, too," says Ben. "I just couldn't believe he'd do it a second time."

A group of regular customers are having a good time in the bar when one of them yells out, "Forty-three." Everyone in the bar goes into fits of laughter. Next, a guy from the other end of the bar says, "Number twenty-three." Again, the bar erupts in laughter. A little while later another voice cries, "How about fifty-six?" And once more the customers in the bar go wild with laughter.

A newcomer in the bar can stand it no longer; he leans across the bar and asks the bartender,

"What's going on? Why does everyone laugh when someone yells out a number?"

"Well," says the bartender "we've all known each other such a long time and we've all heard each other's jokes so often that to save time we gave each joke a number."

A short time later a voice from the back of the bar yells out, "Eighty-nine." This time the choice of numbers is met with dead silence.

The bartender says to the newcomer, "Some people just can't tell a joke."

Harry the bartender is notorious for not allowing any foul language in his establishment when he is tending bar. One evening a couple of strangers come into his place and the first man says to Harry, "Give me a shot of your f——ing whiskey, and make it fast, dammit!"

Harry throws off his apron and comes from around the bar; he knocks the bar stool from under the man, then grabs him by the hair and tosses him out the front door.

Regaining his composure, Harry resumes his place behind the bar and says to the other man, "And what can I get for you?"

"I don't care," he answers. "Just don't pour me any of that f——ing whiskey."

A guy is talking to Smitty. "I got a problem, Smitty. I've been working with the circus cleaning up the animal cages for almost a year now. I smell so bad after work, people won't come near me. And I can barely live on what they pay me."

"Sounds terrible," says Smitty. "Why don't you quit the circus and come and work for me?"

"What," says the guy, "and leave show business?"

An out-of-towner is visiting New York for the first time. He wanders into an uptown bar and strikes up a friendly conversation with the bartender.

"Say," says the stranger, "what's the average tip you get?"

"An average tip, in a place like this, is about ten dollars," answers the bartender.

The man hands over ten dollars. "You must clean up," he says.

"Not really," says the bartender, "this is the first average tip I've gotten this month."

"How come you're late?" asks the bartender as the waitress walks in the door.

"It was awful," she explains. "I was walking down Elm Street and there was this terrible accident. A man was lying in the middle of the street; he was thrown from his car. His leg was broken, his skull was fractured, and there was blood everywhere. Thank God I took that first-aid course; all my training came back to me in a minute."

"What did you do?" asks the bartender.

"I sat down and put my head between my knees to keep from fainting!"

"Say, Bob, how is it that you have seventeen children?" asks the bartender.

"It's because my wife's hard of hearing," explains Bob.

"Now I've heard everything," says the bartender. "How could the fact that your wife is deaf make you have all those kids?"

"It's like this; every night when I go to bed, I ask my wife, 'do you want to go to sleep or what?' And every time she says, 'What?'"

Martha says to the bartender, "The doctor gave me some birth-control pills."

"Birth-control pills?" says the bartender. "Martha, you are eighty years old; why on earth do you need birth-control pills."

"So I can sleep," answers the old lady.

"How do birth-control pills help you sleep?"

"My nineteen-year-old granddaughter lives with me, and every morning I put a pill in her milk. Trust me, I sleep much better!"

Smitty is reading the newspaper and he notices in the obituary column that a very powerful and very unpopular businessman has died. Since the man was a regular customer in Smitty's Bar, he decides to pay his last respects. When he arrives at the funeral, he finds that the church is filled to overflowing.

"My God!" says Smitty to his friend Joe. "I can't believe all the people that are here. How do you explain it?"

"Well," says Joe, "give people what they want and they all show up."

Butch loves to collect antiques for his bar and he gets a good deal on one of those old-fashioned weight machines that tells your weight and your fortune.

After he installs it in his bar, the first person to try it out is one of his grouchy, overweight customers. Butch reads the man's fortune aloud: "You are a kindhearted person, well liked by all who know you."

Then Butch turns the card over, and says, "Wouldn't you know, they got the weight wrong, too."

Three little old ladies are enjoying a glass of wine in their local pub. One of them says, "You know, the strangest things are happening to me. I sometimes find myself at the bottom of my stairway at home and I wonder if I was going upstairs to get something or was coming downstairs to put something away."

The second lady says, "I know what you mean. I'll be standing in front of the refrigerator. I can't for the life of me remember if I just put something in or I'm there to take something out."

The third woman says, "Well, I am happy to report, ladies, that nothing like that has happened to me yet. But I'd better knock on wood"—which she does three times. Then she looks at the other ladies and says as she starts to get up, "Someone's at the door, excuse me!"

A couple of tough-looking bikers burst into Smitty's Bar. In no time at all, they get into an argument with a couple of the regular customers.

Smitty says, "If you guys want to fight, I'm going to have to ask you to step outside."

In just a few minutes, the regulars are back in the bar ordering a beer from Smitty.

"Well," says Smitty, "what happened?"

"Can you believe those guys, they pulled out razors!"

"No kidding?" says Smitty.

"It was okay. They didn't have anyplace to plug them in."

A guy is drinking his beer, looking rather glum. The bartender approaches him and says, "What's the problem, pal?"

"Well, it's like this, my IQ is 200 and I don't have anyone to talk with."

"No problem, let me introduce you to John over here. He's got a high IQ. You'll enjoy talking with him." The bartender introduces them, and before long they are discussing chess, quantum physics, and the abstract-art exhibit at the local museum.

Then the bartender spots another guy who is sitting at the bar. "What can I do for you?" he asks.

"I've got an IQ of 120 and I don't have anyone to talk to."

"No problem," says the bartender. "I'll introduce you to Alex."

In no time, the two men are discussing last week's football game, the newest Schwarzenegger movie, and the recent newspaper strike.

Then the bartender says to another guy sitting at the bar, "What can I do for you?"

"I've got an IQ of 75 and I don't have anyone to talk to."

"I know just the guy who would be perfect for you," says the bartender.

The two men meet and one says to the other, "So how's your reelection campaign going?"

The owner of the Good Times Tavern calls one of his bartenders into the office and says, "Jim, you are a great bartender. You know how to make any drink anyone orders. You always come to work early and make sure your bar is set up flawlessly, and you stay late to make sure everything is spotlessly clean. When you do the liquor ordering, you do it to perfection."

"Boss," says Jim, "does this mean you are giving me a raise?"

"No," says the owner, "you're fired. It's people like you that go out and open your own bars."

A New York theatrical agent is surprised when a bartender in his favorite bar leans across the bar, shakes his hand, and says, "Remember me? I'll bet you're surprised to see me tending bar."

"Not really," says the agent, "I remember your acting."

A man walks into a crowded bar and says, "I want to buy everyone in here a drink, and pour one for yourself, bartender."

His generosity is met with loud approval and the bartender is kept quite busy pouring all the drinks. He pours himself a glass of fine brandy and says to the stranger, "That will be $150."

The man looks him dead in the eye, lifts his glass, and says, "I'm just a little short this week. Put it on my tab and I'll pay you later."

In a rage, the bartender takes the man by the collar and throws him out of the bar. A few minutes later, the man comes back. He takes his place at the bar and announces to the bartender, "Give everyone a drink on me . . . but not for you. Drinking makes you mean."

A couple of partners in a bar found out that their bartender stole $100 from the register. One of the partners wants to fire the bartender on the spot. But the other partner has a more understanding attitude. He says to his partner, "After all, we started on a small scale ourselves."

The bar is packed to the rafters with a group of law students. They are there to watch a trial that is being televised live from the downtown court-room. A hush falls over the crowd. The prosecutor is giving his summation.

"Ladies and gentlemen of the jury, both these men are guilty of engaging in violent acts. The one man had a set of brass knuckles and a .45 automatic. He was wearing a bullet-proof vest. He had, on his person, a knife with a sixteen-inch blade, and in the trunk of his car he had an Uzi. The other man had a sawed-off shotgun and an umbrella with the tip filed down to be as sharp as a razor. He was wearing a steel helmet and he had a flamethrower strapped to his back. These two men were ready for World War III and yet they claim they are innocent victims, just acting in self-defense."

His rousing words stirs the jury and they deliberate for only one hour. When they come back into the courtroom, the judge asks, "What is your verdict?"

The foreman stands and says, "Guilty, Your Honor. But we, the members of the jury, would pay a hundred bucks each if you could arrange for us to see them fight."

One bar manager was forced to fire one of his waitresses. He says to the owner, "She keeps asking me what to do about the simplest problems . . . and it's getting embarrassing to keep saying I don't know."

Mr. Finnigan is celebrating his ninety-fifth birthday at his neighborhood saloon. He blows out the candles on his cake, then he looks down at his hands and says, "Happy birthday, hands, you've been with me all these years, serving me well, and today you are ninety-five."

Then he looks at his feet and says, "Happy birthday, feet, you've lasted all this time taking me from one place to another. Happy ninety-fifth."

And then he looks down at his zipper, sighs, and says, "And you, if you were alive today, you'd be ninety-five, too!"

Two elderly English brothers who live in New York wander into their local pub. Philip pushes his brother Reggie's wheelchair to their usual places at the table near the window. A proper-looking chap comes into the bar.

Philip says in a loud voice, for Reggie is rather deaf, "Look at that man, Reggie, I think he's English."

"Yoo-hoo," says Philip, "I say, are you English?"

"Jolly good," replies the stranger, "born and bred."

"What did he say?" asks the hard-of-hearing Reggie.

"He says he's English," answers Philip. "I say, what part of England are you from?"

"From London," says the man.

"Where?" demands the deaf Reggie.

"He says he's from London," answers Philip. "And what part of London would that be?"

"Just near Hyde Park," answers their fellow countryman.

"Which park?" asks Reggie.

"Hyde Park?" asks Philip. "I say, good fellow, do you know Lady Worthington Farnsworth the Third?"

"That dotty old twit, that good-for-nothing old windbag, that poor excuse for a whore!"

"What did he say?" demands the deaf Reggie.

"Why, he says he knows Mother."

A tavern owner's water pipes burst early one cold Friday morning. He calls a plumber, and after working on the pipes for fifteen minutes, the plumber hands the owner the bill.

"A hundred and five dollars!" he yells. "Why, my doctor only gets eighty-five and he's a specialist."

"That's what I used to get," says the plumber, "when I was a doctor."

John, one of the pub's cantankerous regular customers, is seriously ill and has to be hospitalized. Smitty, the bartender, leaves the bar early one afternoon to visit the old grump.

"Smitty," says John, "you are the only visitor I've had in three weeks. You don't know what this means to me. If I get out of here, I promise, pal, I'll give you ten thousand dollars just as my way of saying thanks."

A month later the grouch shows up at the bar none the worse for wear.

"Glad to see you back," says Smitty, "I guess you've come to make good on your promise of the ten thousand dollars."

"Did I promise you that?" asks John. "Just shows you how sick I really was."

A guy who owns several bars in the city walks into one of his taverns one afternoon. He sees a young man lounging near the bar reading the newspaper. He says to the young man, "How much do you make a week?"

"Oh," says the man, "about two hundred dollars a week."

The owner takes two hundred dollars out of his

wallet, hands it to the guy, and says, "Here's a week's pay. Now get out."

Then the bar manager comes out of the office. The owner asks him, "When did you hire that guy?"

"I didn't," says the manager. "He was waiting for a receipt for the liquor he delivered."

Jim orders six empty beer steins. A puzzled bartender lines up the empty glasses in front of him. Jim takes a hammer from his pocket and one by one smashes the beer steins. The bartender is dumfounded. "What the hell did you do that for?"

"Where I come from, it is customary to break your beer stein when you are drinking with friends," Jim says.

"What friends?" screams the bartender.

"I just picked up a six-pack for me and my buddies. We're meeting at my house. And to tell you the truth, I just hate cleaning up all those little pieces of glass."

Two men walk into a bar. One sits at one end of the bar and the other at the opposite end. The bartender asks the first man what he wants.

"I'll have a Frizzle—that's a beer with a splash of tonic, a splash of orange juice, a squeeze of lemon, no lime."

Then the man at the other end of the bar orders. "Make mine a Frizzle. It's a beer with just a bit of tonic, a bit of orange juice, a squeeze of lemon, but no lime."

The astonished bartender makes the drinks. Then he asks the first man what he does for a living.

"I am a theoretical mathematician at the university."

Then he asks the other man what he does.

"Theoretical mathematician at the college."

"This is remarkable," says the bartender. "You both order a drink that I've never heard of. You have the identical profession and you both walk into my bar on the same day at the same time. What are the odds on something like that happening?"

Both men look up and answer in unison, "Twelve trillion, nine hundred, and eighty-seven billion to one."

Sam is saying to the bartender, "I got serious problems. I live in a house that's worth half a million, I drive a forty-thousand-dollar car, and I'm thinking of buying a lavish summer home in Malibu."

"So," says the bartender, "what's the problem?"

"I only make two hundred dollars a week."

An immigration agent comes into Smitty's Bar looking for illegal employees. They ask the busboy his nationality.

"American," he says.

"American?" says the agent, "Do you know the words to 'The Star-Spangled Banner'?"

"Nope."

"You're an American."

A traveler in Mexico gets lost in a remote area. He stops by a small bar to ask directions. In front of the saloon is an American cowboy riding a beautiful white mare with the Lazy S brand. The traveler says, "That's a fine horse you've got there. If you could rub out that brand, I'd be willing to give you five thousand dollars for her."

The cowboy says, "If I could rub out that mark, I'd still be living in El Paso."

A man walks into a bar carrying a large cardboard box that has air holes poked in the top. Rustling sounds are coming from the box.

"Sorry," says the bartender, "no dogs allowed."

"Isn't a dog."

"Don't allow cats."

"Isn't a cat."

"Well, what the hell is it?"

"It's my brother."

"Who you trying to kid?"

"Honest, we were traveling in Africa and a witch doctor put a curse on—"

"I get it. He shrunk your brother!"

"No, he tripled my size. My brother and I are Pygmies."

One of Smitty's regular bar customers, a cranky old man, dies, and his widow requests that someone from the bar say a few words at his funeral.

The old cuss is not very well liked and no one wants to speak at the funeral. Finally, Smitty hits upon a solution. "Let's draw straws. The one who gets the short straw has to speak."

Bill draws the short straw and all the guys from Smitty's are anxious to hear what he will say. Bill gets up and faces the congregation and says, "His brother was worse."

Clyde has a meeting with his staff. "You have probably heard the rumors that have been going around and I want to set you all straight. It is true that our bar is becoming totally automated."

At this news, everyone starts to protest. Then

Clyde holds up his hand. "I want you all to know that not a single person here will lose his or her job. You will get a paycheck every Friday just like you always have. Nothing will change, you will still get sick pay, full benefits, and you will still participate in our pension plan. Everyone here will be expected to appear for work on Wednesday each week. Wednesday only."

All the employees fall silent for a moment. Then a voice from the back yells out, "What? *Every* Wednesday?"

Old man O'Malley has tended bar at Smitty's for years. He goes to California for his vacation, and while he's there he dies. His body is shipped back home and his friends from the bar are viewing his body at the funeral parlor.

Smitty says, "Doesn't he look great!"

"Yeah," says one of his friends. "I think those two weeks in California did him good."

One of the regulars at Smitty's Bar is telling the other customers of his adventures on his vacation in New Mexico. "It was really something," he says. "Indians to the right of me, Indians to the left of me, Indians in the front, Indians in the back . . ."

"So," says Smitty, "what did you do?"

"What could I do? I bought a blanket."

"What's the matter, friend?" asks the bartender.

"It's like this; two years ago, my grandfather died and left me $80,000," says the man.

"You're upset about that?" asks the bartender.

"Wait," says the man, "then last year, my uncle died and left me $120,000."

"So what's the problem?"

"It's June already," says the man, "and so far not a cent."

Joe has had an especially busy Saturday night tending bar. After he cleans up, counts the money, and locks up, he finally gets to bed at 4:30 A.M.

He is no sooner asleep than his phone rings. The man on the other end says, "What time does the bar open?"

"Ten o'clock," Joe says, and hangs up.

A few minutes later, the phone rings again and the same man asks, "What time does the bar open?"

"I told you, ten o'clock," yells Joe. "I'll let you in then."

"In, hell!" says the man. "I want out."

A man sitting at the bar orders a beer. He is just about to take his first swallow when he sighs and faints dead away. The bartender tries everything he knows to revive him, but with no luck. He looks in the man's pockets, takes out his wallet, and finds out where he lives. He tries to get the man on his feet, but his legs are like rubber. With great effort, he drags the rubber-legged man to his car and drives him home. With a tremendous effort, he hauls the man to his front door. There the man's wife thanks the bartender for bringing her husband home. Just as the bartender is ready to leave, the man's wife says, "What happened to his wheelchair?"

Andy says to the guy sitting at the bar next to him. "I've got problems. I'm head over heels in debt and plagued with bills. I'd give a thousand dollars to anyone who'd do my worrying for me."

"I'll take that deal," says the guy. "Where's my thousand bucks?"

"That's your first worry."

Jeff orders a Manhattan. The bartender puts a frothy drink with a sprig of parsley floating on top in front of him.

"What's this?" asks the bewildered Jeff.

"That's what you ordered, a Manhattan," says the bartender.

"I see," says Jeff, holding up the parsley. "And what's this green thing, Central Park?"

Max rushes into a bar and he says to the bartender, "Quick, give me a drink before the trouble starts."

The bartender gives him one in a hurry and says, "When does the trouble start?"

"Right now," says Max. "I'm broke."

A guy walks into a bar wearing a leopard-skin loincloth. He's carrying a shopping bag that's filled with tiny pieces of string. The man has his face painted like an Indian warrior. He's wearing a beanie with a propeller and he has a pair of huge fuzzy bedroom slippers on his ears. The bartender is about to throw the man out when one of the customers says to him, "Let me handle this, I am a psychiatrist and I've seen cases like this before. I think I can help him.

"Hello there," says the psychiatrist to the man, "I want you to know I am a qualified psychiatrist; you can trust me. Now, what seems to be the problem?"

"Well," says the man, "I'm worried about my brother."

Alice and Betty are sitting at the bar and Betty says to Alice, "Are you having another one?"

"No," Alice says, blushing, "it's just the way my dress is buttoned."

Joel and Craig are watching the latest launch of the Space Shuttle on the evening news in Smitty's Bar.

"Do you think that there is intelligent life on other planets?" says Joel.

"There has to be," says Craig.

"What makes you so sure?"

"Well, for one thing, you don't see them throwing away billions and billions of dollars looking for intelligent life down here!"

It is in the Old West in front of the Lucky Horseshoe Saloon; a prospector is loading up his mule. A guy comes out of the saloon and spots the prospector and thinks he'll have some fun. "Hey, old man," he says, taking out his six-shooter, "do you know how to dance?"

He shoots at the old man's feet. The prospector leans over and takes a double-barreled shot gun from his pack and says, "Have you ever kissed a mule?"

"No," says the young man, "but I've always wanted to."

Mike strikes up a conversation with the bartender. "I've quit my job and taken up writing as a career."

"Sold anything yet?" asks the bartender.

"Oh, yeah, lots of stuff," says Mike.

"Like what?"

"My watch, my TV set, my VCR, my stereo . . ."

Bob and Ray are having a beer in their neighborhood bar and they strike up a conversation.

"It's been one of those weeks," says Bob. "Nothing is going my way."

"I have this great way of handling problems," says Ray. "I carry three sealed envelopes with me that have advice for three emergencies. I open one when I need it. Here, let me give you a set."

Bob takes the envelopes and puts them in his pocket. The next day he has a terrible fight with his neighbor and he opens the first envelope. It says, "Blame yourself for this mess." He takes the advice, apologizes to his neighbor, and straightens it all out.

The next day nothing is going right at work and he opens the second envelope. It says, "Blame the office computer." He blames the computer and the boss gives him the rest of the day off.

The next day on the way home from work Bob is held up at gunpoint. The thug takes his wallet with all his credit cards. Bob opens the third envelope. It says, "Call the cops, then prepare three more envelopes."

In the Old West, a man walks into a saloon and says, "I've got three unmarried daughters, all of 'em ugly. If one of you varmints marries them, I'll pay one thousand dollars for the twenty-five-year-old, and I'm willing to pay five thousand for the thirty-year-old. For the forty-year-old, I'll pay ten thousand, but she's awful fat and she's got no teeth."

One guy at the end of the bar says, "Have you got one about fifty-five?"

A well-dressed man walks into a bar and orders himself a beer. The bartender hands him the bottle and the man hands the bartender the bottle cap as payment.

"What's going on?" says the bartender.

"Don't worry," says the man. "Keep track of the caps and I'll pay you at the end of the evening."

The man is there for hours, buying beers for everyone in the bar. Finally, it comes time for him to leave and he says to the bartender, "Okay, how many bottle caps?"

"There's fifty-five caps total," says the bartender.

"No problem," says the man. "Do you have change for a manhole cover?"

A cowboy walks into the saloon and yells out, "Where's the man who painted my horse green?"

A guy at the end of the bar stands up; he is six-foot-eight and weighs about three hundred pounds. "I painted your broken-down old nag. What of it?"

"I just wanted you to know that the first coat is dry."

Joe has a drink in a bar and leaves the waitress a tip of three dimes. The next night he comes in again and the waitress says to him, "I can tell your fortune by the tip you left last night."

"Really," says Joe, "tell me."

"All three dimes were in a row, which shows you are neat," says the waitress. "And the first dime shows you are thrifty. The second dime shows that you are a bachelor."

"What does the third dime show?" asks Joe.

"That dime shows that your father was a bachelor, too."

Sam is complaining to the bartender that his shoes are too tight and they are killing him. The bartender says, "So why don't you buy a bigger pair?"

"It's like this," says Sam. "I hate my job, all my wife and I do is fight. I'm eighty thousand dollars in debt, my son is in jail, and my daughter has five kids, she just divorced her husband and moved back in with us. So when I go to bed at night and take off my shoes, it's the only pleasure I get all day."

A group from the United Nations are having a drink at a nearby New York bar. One of the delegates says to the group, "Pardon me, but what's your opinion of the food shortage?"

The delegate from Quebec says, "What shortage?"

The delegate from Moscow says, "What's food?"

The delegate from Havana says, "What's an opinion?"

And the delegate from New York says, "What's 'pardon me'?"

A lumberjack walks into a saloon carrying a large ax. He says to the bartender, "I'd like a drink, but all I have is this ax."

"No problem," says the bartender. He pours the guy a drink. When the lumberjack is finished, he hands the bartender the ax and starts to leave the saloon.

"Just a minute," says the bartender, and he hands the guy a hatchet. "You forgot your change."

Larry and Moe are drinking a beer in a bar. Larry says to Moe, "What would happen if you cut off one of your ears?"

"I guess I'd lose some of my hearing."

"Well," says Larry, "what would happen if you cut off both of your ears?"

"I guess I'd go blind."

"Why the hell would you go blind if you cut off your ears?"

"Because if I cut off my ears, my hat would fall down over my eyes and I couldn't see."

Three college students walk into a bar and order three beers. The bartender looks at them and says, "I'll have to see some IDs."

Two of the guys show the bartender their driver's licenses and the third guy says, "Gee, I forgot my license. Will my library card do?"

The bartender nods and says, "Okay, that'll be two drafts and a book."

There's a bar full of people when an earthquake hits and everything starts to shake. One of the customers yells out, "Don't panic! I'm from San Francisco and the best place to stand is in a doorway."

Everyone runs for the door. One guy is standing in the middle of the bar. He says, "I'm from Chicago. What the hell do I do?"

A couple of kids are playing cowboys and Indians. They walk into the pretend saloon and the first little boy says to the bartender, "I'll have a shot of rye."

The second little boy says, "And I'll have a whole wheat."

Chuck is feeling depressed; he asks the bartender to call him a cab so he can drive down to the bridge and jump off. When the cabbie arrives, he sizes up the situation and decides to try a little psychology on the guy.

"How much money you got?" asks the cabdriver.

"Six bucks," says Chuck.

"It'll cost you seven to get to the bridge. Sorry, I can't take you," says the cabbie.

"Oh, cabdriver," says a customer at the bar. "Here's a buck, take him!"

Three guys are in a bar—an Englishman, an American, and a Scot. Each of the men discovers that there is a fly in his drink. The Englishman demands that the bartender take the glass back and make him a new drink.

The American picks out the fly and drinks it down without saying a word.

The Scot picks up the fly by the wings and says, "Spit it out . . . spit it out!"

Mike is talking to the bartender. "Yeah," says Mike, "it was great, I went on a whirlwind trip to Europe. I bought a new car and a completely new wardrobe. I was living the life of Riley."

"So what happened?"

"Well," says Mike, "Riley reported his credit cards missing."

A guy is saying to the bartender, "I think the greatest invention in the twentieth century is the thermos bottle."

"You gotta be kidding," says the bartender. "The airplane was invented in this century, not to mention the computer, and what about nuclear energy? And you pick the thermos, a bottle that keeps things hot or cold."

"But that's why it's so great," says the man. "How does it know, how does it know?"

Ernie walks into Smitty's Bar and says, "I just had the worst day; I was driving home from work in rush-hour traffic and I hear *thump . . . thump . . . thump*. A flat tire. I pull over and change the tire, get back into the traffic, and wouldn't you know—*thump . . . thump . . . thump*."

"Wow," says Smitty, "another flat tire! What are the odds on that?"

"Actually," says Ernie, "the first time I changed the wrong tire."

It's forty below zero one winter night in Fairbanks, Alaska. Pat is drinking at his local saloon and the bartender says to him, "You owe me quite a bit on your tab."

"Sorry," says Pat, "I'm flat broke this week."

"That's okay," says the bartender, "I'll just write your name and the amount you owe me right here on the wall."

"But," says Pat, "I don't want any of my friends to see that."

"They won't," says the bartender, "I'll just hang your parka over it until it's paid."

A stranger walks into a bar and starts to pick a fight with one of the regular customers. The bouncer picks him up and throws him into the street. A few minutes later, the guy comes back and the bouncer again picks him up and tosses him outside. Once more, the guy stumbles back into the bar and the bouncer grabs him.

One of the customers looks up and says, "Your

problem is you're putting too much backspin on him."

Carl orders a glass of whiskey. He takes a sip of his drink and spits it out. "This stuff is terrible," he says to the bartender.

"I don't know what you are complaining about," says the bartender, "you only got a shot. I've got ten cases of the stuff."

The guys in Smitty's are watching the end of the football game when someone accidentally switches the channel to the ballet on the PBS station. One guy looks up at the dancers whirling around on their toes and says, "If they want tall girls, why don't they hire tall girls?"

A native is talking to a beautiful young woman in a bar on a remote tropical island.

"Look at it this way," he says. "Next time the chief decides to sacrifice a virgin, you won't have a thing to worry about."

A bartender loses his life savings investing in the stock market. He is crushed and decides to take his life. He is just about to jump out the window when he hears a voice: "Don't jump."

The bartender says, "Why not, I've lost everything!"

The voice says, "Borrow a hundred dollars, and buy soybeans."

The bartender is skeptical but borrows the money and buys the soybeans. The next day soybeans quadruple. That night the voice comes back and says, "Reinvest, buy more soybeans." The bartender does it and again the price of soybeans shoots up.

This goes on every day for weeks until the man has $500,000. The voice says, "Stop . . . that's all I can do for you."

But the bartender can't resist and the next day he invests everything he's got in the soybean market. He loses his fortune. Again he's about to jump out the window. He says out loud, "What should I do now?"

The voice comes back and says, "Jump out the window."

Mr. Perkins walks into a bar and sits down on one of the stools. "Can I get you a drink?" asks the bartender.

"No thanks," says Mr. Perkins. "I tried drinking once and didn't like it."

A few minutes pass and the bartender lights up a cigar. "Care for a smoke?" asks the bartender.

"No, thank you," says Mr. Perkins. "I tried smoking once and I didn't much care for it."

The guys want to play a game of poker in the back room and they ask the guy at the bar if he wants to join them.

"No thanks," says Mr. Perkins. "I tried gambling once and it just wasn't for me."

The man just sits there at the end of the bar and finally the bartender says to him, "You don't drink, you don't smoke, and you don't gamble. What are you doing here?"

"I am here to meet my son."

"He must be," says the bartender, "an only child."

"Hey, Smitty, can I bum a cigarette?"

"I thought you quit."

"I'm in phase one of quitting."

"What's phase one?"
"I quit buying."

A dishonest bar owner puts an ad in the newspaper looking for an accountant. He has the field narrowed down to three applicants to be interviewed. The first guy comes in and the owner says to him, "How much is two and two?" He says "Four." The owner says, "Thanks," and they call in the next applicant. She also answers, "Four" to the question. Then the last applicant comes in. The owner says "How much is two and two?"

The guy thinks for a minute, then he says, "How much do you want it to be?"

The owner says, "You're hired!"

A successful bar owner is scolding his son. "When I was your age, I worked sixteen hours a day. I built this bar with my own hands and I've never had a day off in thirty years."

His son says, "Thanks, Dad; if it weren't for your hard work and dedication ... I might have to do that myself."

The Goat's Head Pub is noted for its fine food. One day a cranky old man comes in and orders a roast-beef sandwich. He eats the sandwich and then demands to see the manager. "I have a complaint," the old man says. "This is the worst roast-beef sandwich I have ever had. There's too much fat on the meat and the bread is tasteless and the lettuce is limp. I wouldn't eat this slop if I were starving. And to make matters worse, you serve such small portions."

Charlie walks into Smitty's and is frantically searching all over the bar."

"Hey," says Smitty, "what's going on?"

"I lost my wallet," says Charlie.

"So you're looking for your wallet."

"No," says Charlie. "My buddy Bill found my wallet."

"Great," says Smitty, "so what are you looking for now?"

"Bill."

A beautiful redhead is sitting at the bar and a guy says to her, "How about you and I go out in my car and make out."

"That'll be the day," says the woman.

"Okay, then how about we go to my apartment and we get it on?"

"That'll be the day," says the woman.

"Well then, how would you like to take a ride in my Learjet and we fly to my private villa on the Italian Riviera?"

The woman looks at him and says, "This'll be the day."

"Hey, Smitty," says one of the guys at the bar, "I got a great Christmas bonus from work this week."

"What are you going to do with it?"

"Well," he says, "my wife wants a fur coat, but I want a new car."

"What are you going to do?" asks Smitty.

"Oh, we reached a compromise," says the guy. "We are going to buy the fur coat, but I'm keeping it in the garage."

Ken walks into a bar, sits down, and orders a beer.

"Excuse me," says a man sitting next to him, "I couldn't help but notice what beautiful teeth you have. I'm looking for a good dentist; who did your work?"

"Actually, he's a new dentist and he works very cheaply."

"And you've been happy with the results?"

"I have a hobby."

"I'm sure you do, but I'm more interested in your teeth."

"My hobby relates to my teeth. Every morning about 6:00 A.M., I go swimming in the nude at a secluded spot down by the ocean."

"What's that got to do with your teeth?"

"Wait, I'll tell you. I went down to the ocean yesterday, just as I do every day, and I was taking off my clothes and I saw this beautiful woman. She was a goddess, and not wearing a thing. At first, I was embarrassed, but she was perfectly at ease. She kept walking toward me and finally our bodies touched."

"So what's that got to do with your teeth?" asks the man.

"For the first time in six months my teeth stopped hurting."

A guy goes into a bar-supply shop and says to the owner, "I understand my boss, Frank, has owed you for a dozen leather bar stools for three years now."

"Yeah," says the store owner, "are you here to make good on the account?"

"No," says the guy, "I wanted to buy some on the same terms!"

A ship goes down, the only survivor's lifeboat washes ashore on a remote island. A tribe of cannibals capture him and tie him to a stake. For the next several weeks, they proceed to nick his arms with their spears and drink his blood. Finally, he can't take it anymore.

He calls the chief and says, "Let me go or kill me, but this has got to stop. I'm tired of being stuck for the drinks."

3

SPIN THE BOTTLE

Across the crowded bar, your eyes meet. You elbow your way through the crowd. Finally, the two of you are together and you say those three magic words ... "Who's your friend?" We take an irreverent look at the lighter side of love.

Dan is ready to leave the bar and he asks the bartender how much he owes him.

"That'll be twenty-five cents," says the bartender.

"How can that be?" asks Dan. "I had two drinks and I bought a bottle of French champagne for that couple celebrating their anniversary."

"I know," says the bartender. "But when the owner's not here, I charge whatever I want."

"Where is the owner?"

"He's upstairs with my wife. He's doing to her up there what I am doing to him down here."

Tim and his wife, Patty, own a tavern. During football season, it is almost impossible to drag Tim away from the television.

"Honey," says Patty, "you really need to get into the liquor room and wash down the walls."

Not taking his eyes from the television, Tim says, "So who am I, Mr. Clean?"

The next day Patty says, "Tim, the beer cooler isn't working right."

Tim is totally engrossed in the fourth quarter of the game and says, "So who am I, Mr. Fixit?"

The next day Tim says, "I know I haven't been very helpful around the bar lately. I'll do anything you want."

"Forget it," Patty says. "I had Bill the bartender do it all.'"

"What did you give him?" asks Tim.

"Well," she says, "Bill said I could either bake him a cake or sleep with him."

"What kind of cake did you make?"

"So who am I, Betty Crocker?"

"I just got a letter today. It said, 'I know you have been fooling around with my wife. Please call my lawyer's office and we will discuss this matter.' "

The bartender says, "What are you going to do?"

"Simple," says the guy. "I'll just write back, 'Received your chain letter. Delighted to attend the meeting.' "

A woman goes to the doctor. She's upset because she and her husband haven't been able to have a baby. The doctor tells her, "You are putting too much pressure on yourselves. Just forget about it. Don't pay attention to the time of month when you make love, don't take your temperature. I recommend in these cases that you just relax and make love whenever the mood strikes you."

Several months later, the woman comes back to the doctor and the tests show that she's pregnant. The doctor says to her, "Did you take my advice?"

"Oh, doctor, we did. It was so romantic. It was a hot afternoon, we were just sitting at the table having a beer. I looked at Henry and he looked at me and we ripped off our clothes and made mad passionate love right there under the table."

"You must be very happy."

"I am, doctor, except for one thing."

"What's that?"

"They won't let us into Smitty's Bar anymore."

A young man nervously approaches his girl-friend's father one evening. He says, "Sir, I have something very important ... that is, I was wondering if ... that is, I'd like to know if I could—"

The father interrupts him. "You want to marry my daughter. You are a fine young man and you come from a good family. I would be happy to give you my blessing."

"That's not it," says the young man. "You see my car payment is coming up and I'm a little short this month and I was just wondering if you could ..."

"Certainly not! I hardly know you."

Nineteen-year-old Larry is in a drugstore; he's lingering near the prescription department and just can't work up the nerve to talk to the female pharmacist.

Finally, sensing his discomfort, the lady druggist says to him, "Is there something I can help you with?"

"Er ... ah ... no ... it isn't important." And with that, Larry turns to leave.

"Young man, I've been a trained pharmacist for twenty years. My sister and I have worked here since we were teenagers. Believe me, there is nothing you can say that will shock us; we are trained professionals."

"Okay," says Larry, "it's like this. I have an insatiable sexual appetite. Nothing seems to appease me. No matter how often I make love, I just want more and more. All I think about is sex, sex, sex. Is there anything you can give me?"

"Let me confer with my sister."

After a few minutes, she comes back and says, "The best we can offer," she says, "is five hundred a week and half interest in the business."

A young actress finally gets her big break and is cast in a movie with a speaking part. It is a low-budget movie and they can't pay for a stand-in for the actress. The first day on the set, the script calls for her to be thrown from a runaway horse and tossed off the top of a three-story building. The next day she is set on fire and almost drowns in a raging river. On the third day of shooting, she is caught in the middle of a buffalo stampede and shot at with bows and arrows.

She manages to drag herself into the director's office and says, "Tell me, who do I have to sleep with to get *out* of this movie?"

Bill and Bob have tended bar together for years. One day Bill says, "I love my wife, but sometimes I get bored. Tell me, have you ever thought of switching? Who says you have to be with your wife and I have to be with my wife all the time!"

Bob says, "Hey, that's a great idea. Let's talk to our wives and see what they think."

Each of them talks to his wife, and much to their delight the wives agree to the plan.

The next morning Bob says to Bill, "How was it for you?"

Bill says, "I had a lot of fun, we should do this again."

"That's what I think," says Bob. "Let's go next door and see how the girls made out."

Fred decides to close his tavern during the Christmas holidays so that he can go skiing with his buddy Duffy. They load up Fred's station wagon and head north. After driving for a few hours, they get caught in a terrible blizzard. They drive into a nearby farmhouse and ask the beautiful young lady of the house if they can spend the night.

"I'm not sure it would be proper," she explains. "I am recently a widow and don't want the neighbors to talk."

"You don't have a thing to worry about," says Fred. "We'll stay in the barn."

Nine months later, Fred gets a letter from the widow. When Duffy comes into the bar, Fred confronts him.

"Duffy, do you remember that widow at the farm?"

"Yes," says Duffy.

"Did you by any chance get up in the middle of the night and go to the house?"

"Yeah, I gotta admit it."

"And did you and the widow by any chance become intimate?"

"Okay, okay, we did."

"And did you use my name?"

Duffy turns red and says, "Yeah, I did."

"Well, thanks, pal . . . she just died and left me her farm."

A young woman walks into an overcrowded bar. She can't find a seat anywhere. Finally, she leans over and says to a guy sitting on a bar stool, "Excuse me, but I'm pregnant, can I have your seat?"

The guy stands up to offer her his seat and he notices that she's very slim. "How long have you been pregnant?"

"Oh," she says, "about half an hour."

Frank meets a very attractive young woman in his local bar. They talk for hours and Frank is delighted that they have so much in common. They both love the theater, they both play golf, and they both have season tickets for the Giants. Frank is overjoyed when she invites him home with her.

She takes him to her high-rise apartment with a view of the San Francisco Bay. When she opens the door, there in the middle of the living-room floor is the body of a dead horse.

The woman, noticing the look of horror on Frank's face, says, "Well, I never said I was neat!"

A young woman is in her psychiatrist's office discussing her dreams. "Dr. Floyd, I don't think I know what you mean when you say my dreams are filled with phallic symbols."

"Well, my dear," says the psychiatrist, "a phallic symbol is anything that can be used to represent a phallus."

"But, doctor," says the young woman, "what is a phallus?"

"I'll show you," says the doctor as he unzips his pants.

"I get it," she says. "It's just like a man's thing but much, much smaller."

Ralph is complaining to the bartender: "When I first got married, my wife would bring me the paper and the dog would run around barking at me. And let me tell you, after ten years, things have changed. Now the dog brings me the paper and my wife barks at me."

"What are you complaining about?" says the bartender. "You're getting the same service."

Three guys from Smitty's Bar decide to go camping for the weekend. They are just an hour from their campsite when their car breaks down. They walk over to a farmhouse and ask the farmer if they can spend the night. The farmer has a beautiful teenage daughter, so he's a little reluctant. "You fellas can sleep upstairs in the attic. I'll be in my room with a loaded shotgun by my side. If I hear you come down the stairs, I'll shoot you," says the farmer.

Bill, John, and Duffy agree to stay in the attic and they go to sleep. In the middle of the night, Bill wakes up and has to use the bathroom. As he makes his way down the stairs he hears the farmer getting out of bed and cocking his shotgun. The farmer yells, "Who's there?"

Bill says, "Meow ... meow." The farmer thinks it is his pet cat and goes back to bed.

A little while later, John has to use the bathroom and he creeps down the stairs. The farmer grabs his shotgun, jumps out of bed, and yells, "Who's that?"

"Meow," says John. Again, the farmer thinks it is the cat and goes back to bed.

A short time later, Duffy has the same need. He softly walks down the stairs. The farmer pops out of bed and cocks his gun. "Who's there?" he yells.

Duffy says, "It's the cat."

Mr. Smith and Miss Jones are both attending a convention in a large city. They arrive at the hotel and discover through some mix-up that they are registered together in the same room. The hotel is totally booked and there is no hope that they can each have their own room. Resigned to their fate, they decide to share the room.

Each of them chooses a bed and politely ignores the other. During the night, Miss Jones wakes up and says, "Mr. Smith, would you mind getting up and getting me the extra pillow from the closet?"

Mr. Smith says, "Look, we're both adults. How about if we act like we are man and wife?"

Miss Jones says, "Well, actually, I've been thinking the same thing."

"Great," he says. "Then get up and get your own damn pillow."

Bill and his wife are staying in a hotel; when he checks out, he complains to the manager about the cost of the room. The manager explains that that was the normal cost for a double room with a bath and television.

Bill says, "But we didn't use the television."

"Sorry, but it was there if you wanted to use it!" replies the manager.

"Well, in that case, I am going to charge you for making love to my wife," says the man.

The manager protests. "I never made love to your wife."

"But she was there if you wanted to," answers Bill.

The manager is so confused he reduces the man's hotel bill.

The next time Bill and his wife are staying in a hotel, he tries the same tactic again.

"Sir, that's our normal rate for a double room with a television," says the clerk.

"But I didn't use the television," says Bill.

"It was there if you wanted it," answers the clerk.

"Then I am going to charge you for making love to my wife!"

"Okay," says the hotel clerk, "but don't tell my boss. I'm new here and I don't want to get fired."

A very attractive woman is sitting in a bar. A guy approaches her and says, "May I buy you a drink?"

She says, "I am not that kind of girl."

He says, "Don't get me wrong, I just want to talk, I don't mean anything by it."

They are talking and the man says, "How would you like to go for a ride in my new car?"

"You don't understand, I am not that kind of girl," is her answer.

"I know you're not," says the man. "I just want to get out of here and get some air, why don't you come along?"

They are driving around in his car, having a great time, when the man says, "We're near my apartment, why don't you come up for a while?"

"I've told you before, I am not that kind of girl!"

The man says, "I know, I know. I don't mean anything. I just want you to see my place."

The woman agrees, and they are sitting on his couch and he says, "Would you like to see my bedroom?"

She says, "How many times do I have to tell you? I am not that kind of girl."

He says, "You don't understand. I want you for my wife."

She says, "Great! Where is she?"

A young man knocks on the door of a well-known madam. She shows him inside and he says to her, "I want a blonde about twenty-five, but I have an unusual need. . . ."

"No need to explain," says the madam. "Our girls are the most skilled in the city. They will give you complete satisfaction."

"But," says the man, "you don't understand. I want special treatment. . . ."

"Don't worry. Bonita will take good care of you. She's an expert in special cases."

Bonita and the young man go upstairs; in no time the young man comes downstairs again.

"Excuse me," he says, "Bonita won't agree to—"

"Won't? One of my girls won't do something? This is not tolerated in my house. Nothing is more important to me than a satisfied client. I will see to it that you have what you want. I will take care of you myself. Tell me what is it you want?"

"Well," he says, "I want it on credit."

A bartender is working at a catered party in the home of a wealthy married couple. He is getting the bar set up before the party begins and the wife takes him aside and invites him into her bedroom. The bartender believes in mixing business with pleasure, and in a matter of minutes they are making mad passionate love.

The next day the bartender's home phone rings; it is the wealthy married woman. "My husband is out playing golf," she says, "come on over."

"What," says the bartender, "on my own time?"

Alex has to travel a lot for his business. He is married to a beautiful young blonde and is suspicious that she isn't alone when he is out of town.

The thought that she may be with another man is driving him crazy. But he isn't sure. He is finally forced to hire a private detective.

He is out of town for two weeks, and when he gets back, he immediately calls the detective. "Tell me, I want to know everything. It's that element of doubt that's just driving me crazy."

"Are you sitting down?" asks the detective. "It doesn't look good. The day you left, a good-looking guy comes over to your house early in the morning. Your wife comes out with the man and they got in his convertible. I follow them in my car. They go to a nude beach. They are kissing and frolicking in the water all day. After that, they come back to your house. I was watching through the window. They walk into the bedroom, kiss, and then they turn out the lights and I couldn't see any more."

"That's what I mean," says the man. "There's that element of doubt again!"

A woman meets a guy in a bar. She notices that his tie has the design of a whip and handcuffs on it. He offers to give her a ride in his new car. As she opens the door, there on the passenger seat is a pair of handcuffs and a whip. The man tosses them into the backseat without a word of explanation. They go to his apartment; she sees that there is a huge portrait of a man dressed in black leather with a whip in one hand and a pair of handcuffs in the other. The man excuses himself and goes into the bedroom to change. When he comes out, he's dressed in black leather and he says to her, "Now I'm going to make love to you."

She says, "Thank God!"

Mr. and Mrs. Wagner are at their doctor's office for their annual checkup. Mr. Wagner goes in first and the doctor asks him if he has any complaints.

"Just one, doctor; the first time I make love to my wife, everything is great, and the second time I get all sweaty."

"I'm sure there is nothing to worry about," the doctor reassures him.

Next, Mrs. Wagner goes in to see the doctor. During her examination, the doctor says to her, "Your husband mentioned that the first time you make love, everything is fine, and the second time he's all sweaty. Why do you think that is?"

"Because," Mrs. Wagner says, "the first time it's December and the second time it's July."

A married woman in her twenties and a married woman in her seventies are sitting next to each other in a bar waiting for their husbands to join them. They strike up a conversation and are talking about a recent episode of Donohue they had both seen on television. The "Donohue Show" had a sex therapist on who described how the sex lives of married couples changes over the years. The younger woman says to the older, "I hope you don't think I'm prying, but do you and your husband have mutual orgasms?"

"No," says the older lady with a blush, "we have State Farm."

Bruce the bartender suspects that his wife is seeing another man. One day he deliberately comes home from work early. His wife is wearing a sexy nightgown and he smells cigar smoke. Bruce goes through his house in a rage—looking under the bed, searching all the closets, and turning over all the furniture.

Finally, he pulls back the shower curtain and

there, standing in the shower, is a man wearing only his underwear.

"What the hell are you doing here?" demands the husband.

"Everyone's got to be somewhere."

Hank comes home after stopping at his local bar for a drink and finds his wife in bed with another man. He rushes out of the room, yelling, "I am going to get my gun."

His wife comes running after him, saying, "Please don't. You don't know what you are doing! It was my lover that paid for our new car. He was the one who gave me the money so we could take that trip to Hawaii. I don't really have a part-time job. All that extra money came from him."

Hank just ignores her.

"Please, don't get your gun," she cries.

"What gun?" Hank says. "I am getting a blanket; that poor guy could get pneumonia lying there like that."

Dr. Smith is examining his first patient, an elderly man who isn't feeling very well. After an extensive work-up, the young doctor says, "Mr. Jones, in general you are in good health for a man your age, but there is one thing. I would suggest . . . that is . . . maybe you should . . . that is to say . . . perhaps you could give up some of your love life."

Mr. Jones thinks for a long while and then says, "Sounds okay to me, doc. But which half do I give up—thinking about it or talking about it?"

A guy is standing trial for killing his wife. He is claiming temporary insanity. The judge asks the guy to take the stand and describe what happened the night of the murder.

"Well, Your Honor, it was like this. I am normally a peaceful man who has a regular schedule. I never bother anyone. I get up every day precisely at seven o'clock, go to work and punch in at nine, and leave work at five. I come home at six and find dinner ready for me. After dinner, I watch TV until ten, then I go to bed.

"My routine never varies. Up at seven, work at nine, dinner at six, bed at ten. Day after day after day. It's always the same. Until the day in question."

"And on the day in question?" asks the judge.

"On that day," the man continues, "I got up at seven and went to work at nine, left work at five, and came home at six, just like always. But on that night, there was no dinner on the table and my wife was nowhere in sight. I searched the house and found her in bed with another man. So I killed her."

"And what exactly were you thinking when you killed her?"

"I went insane," says the man. "I didn't know what I was doing, I couldn't control myself." He turns to the judge and says in a passionate voice, "When I come home at six o'clock, dinner better be on the table."

Bill's wife died and he is weeping at her grave-side during the funeral services.

"Bill, Bill," says one of his friends, "I know it seems terrible now, but just remember that time will take away the pain. Who knows—in a year or two you could meet another woman and maybe get married."

Bill dries his eyes and says, "A year or two? What am I going to do tonight?"

Old lady Biddy comes home early from her bridge game one afternoon and she finds her eighty-year-old husband in bed with their sexy twenty-two-year-old neighbor. The older woman is so outraged that she picks up her husband and throws him out the fifth-story window and he falls to his death.

When Mrs. Biddy is brought before the judge, he shakes his head in disbelief. "How could you throw your husband out the window?" he asks.

"Judge," the old lady says, "when I saw him with that young girl, doing what he was doing, I figured, if he could do that, he could fly."

Jane is in the process of getting a divorce and is meeting with her attorney. The lawyer is explaining to her the concept of community property.

"You understand that your property must be divided equally, don't you?" the lawyer asks her.

"You mean that ten thousand dollars I've saved up—I have to give him half?"

"That's right," says the lawyer.

"What about the furniture?" asks Jane.

"You will have to work out a plan to divide it equally. Maybe he could have the dining-room-and-kitchen furniture and you could take the living-room-and-bedroom things."

"Well," asks Jane, "what about the three children?"

That has the lawyer stumped. "How about this? Go back and live with him for a while, have another baby, then you take two and he can have two."

"I don't think so," answers Jane. "If I depended on him, I wouldn't have the three I got!"

Back in the Wild West an Indian chief is standing outside the saloon. Each time an attractive woman walks by, he says, "Chance."

One of the cowboys leaving the saloon can't help but notice the Indian chief. Finally, his curiosity gets the best of him and he says, "Chief, how come you say 'chance' when you see a pretty lady? I thought you said, 'how.'"

"I know how—just want chance."

Rod checks into a New York hotel. He opens the door to his room and finds a pair of beautiful twenty-one-year-old naked twins stretched out on the bed.

"Surprise," the twins say in unison, "we're a gift from your friend Bill."

"Young ladies," says Rod, "I am one of the most respected men in my field. I have been married for twenty years. I have a wonderful family that I love very much. I have never been touched by a word of scandal; my good name is above reproach. I am sorry, but one of you will have to leave!"

Two accountants, Henry and Ben, are the best of friends. They both work together and are close to retirement. One day they are having a drink together after work, and Henry says to Ben, "Last night I made love to my wife three times."

Ben says, "Three times? How did you do it?"

Henry tells him, "I read about it in a book. I made love to my wife, then I rolled over and took a ten-minute nap. I woke up, I made love to her again, then rolled over and took another ten-minute nap. Woke up, made love to her again, and then I went to sleep. This morning I woke up feeling like I was eighteen."

Ben says, "This is wonderful. I have to try it!" He goes home that night and goes to bed. He makes love to his wife and rolls over and takes a ten-minute nap. He wakes up, makes love to his wife, and then takes another ten-minute nap. He wakes up again and makes love to his wife and falls asleep. He wakes up in the morning and he's twenty minutes late for work. He throws on his clothes and catches the bus for work.

When Ben gets to the office, the boss is waiting for him. "Boss, I'm sorry. I've been working here for twenty-five years and I've never been late before. Please forgive me for being late these twenty minutes."

The boss says, "Twenty minutes? Where were you on Wednesday and Thursday?"

A guy is away on a business trip and returns home earlier than expected. He gets home and discovers his wife in bed with his best friend.

He says, "Bill! I am married to the lady, so I have to. But you?"

Frank has been out of town on a business trip for three months. On his first night back, he is feeling romantic and suggests to his wife that they make love.

"Oh, honey," says his wife, "you know I love you, but I am so worn-out tonight, the kids just ran me ragged."

The next night Frank tries again with his wife. "Wouldn't you know it," says the wife, "tonight I have the world's worst headache. How about if I give you a rain check?"

By the third night Frank is beside himself and he asks his wife in a rather impatient tone, "Well, how about tonight?"

His wife snaps back, "This is the third night in a row you've asked. I think you've turned into some kind of a sex maniac!"

Tony is having a rough time in his business. One night over dinner, he says to his wife, "You know if I only had as little as two thousand dollars in cash right now, it would make all the difference in my business."

"Is that all it would take?" asks his wife. "Then wait right here."

She runs into the bedroom and comes out with a pickle jar filled with bills. "I've had this secret bank since we've been married. Each time we made love, I put ten dollars in the jar. I bet I've got three thousand dollars in here. It's all yours."

Tony can't believe his eyes. Then he says, "Just think if I had given you all my business."

Two guys are walking in the park when they come across two dogs in the heat of passion.

"Hey, did you ever try that with your wife?" asks the one guy.

"Can't say that I have," says the other guy.

"Me either, but it looks like fun."

"Tell you what, let's both try it, and when we get together next week at Smitty's Bar, we will compare notes."

The next week they both show up at Smitty's.

"So how did it go?" asks one man.

"It was okay," says the other.

"You mean your wife didn't put up a fuss?"

"Why should she?"

"I can't understand it. I promised my wife a trip to Hawaii and she still wouldn't come out to the park."

Rosie, a little old lady, goes to the doctor and says, "Doctor, it's my husband. He is losing his potency and I want to know the cause. Is it mental or is it something physical?"

The doctor is amazed. "Pardon me for asking, but how old are you?"

"Next week I'll be eighty."

"And how old is your husband?" asks the doctor.

"He is eighty-eight."

"Well, tell me this—when did you first notice that he was losing his potency?"

"The first time I noticed was last night, and what scares me is I noticed it again this morning."

A guy is sitting in a bar having a drink when another guy sits down beside him and says, "Are you Joe Wells?"

"Yeah, that's me."

"Were you in San Francisco a few weeks ago?"

"As a matter of fact I was."

"Did you stay at the Fairmont Hotel?"

"Sure did."

"Did you know Jane Smith, who was staying there, too?"

"Yeah, I know Jane."

"Did you have an affair with her?"

"I did."

"Well, I don't like it."

"You know, neither did I."

Bill, recuperating from a long illness, is sitting in Smitty's Bar.

"We've got a great corned-beef sandwich on the menu today," says Smitty.

"No thanks, Smitty," says Bill. "The doctor tells me I've got to watch what I eat."

"Really?"

"He said I can't eat fatty foods and I should get plenty of rest. He also said I should start a regular program of exercise, but nothing too strenuous."

"Tell me," says Smitty, "can you make love?"

"Yeah," said Bill, "but only to my wife. My doctor doesn't want me to get too excited."

A seventy-year-old millionaire announces his engagement to an eighteen-year-old girl in Smitty's Bar. "Drinks are on me," the man says.

"Tell me," says Smitty, "I know you've got money. But how did you get a beautiful eighteen-year-old to marry you when you're seventy?"

"I told her I was ninety-five."

A forgetful man checks out of a hotel. Then he realizes he has left his umbrella behind. He goes back to the hotel room to get it, but the room has been rented already. He listens at the door.

He hears a man's voice saying, "Whose little sweetie are you?"

He hears a woman's voice: "Your little sweetie."

"Whose little hands are these?"

"Your little hands."

"And whose little feet are these . . . and whose little ankles . . . and whose little knees?"

Finally, the man calls through the door, "When you get to the umbrella, it's mine."

Gus, an eighty-year-old man, opens the door to his apartment and finds a beautiful young girl stealing his money.

Gus says, "I'm calling the police."

She says, "Please, mister, I'll be sent away for years if I'm arrested again. Please don't call the police."

Gus says, "I have to."

She pleads, "I'll do anything. You can have my body."

Guy says, "Get in bed."

The two of them are in bed and the old man tries and tries, but nothing happens. Finally, he gives up.

"It's no use," Gus says, "I can't do it. I'll have to call the police."

Will is crawling in the desert, and out of nowhere there's a guy with briefcase. Will, in a weak voice, says, "Water . . . water . . ."

The man says, "In this briefcase, I have the finest selection of neckties you've ever seen for only twenty dollars."

"Water . . . water . . ."

"They'd cost at least twenty-five in any of your downtown stores."

"For God's sake, give me water . . . water . . ."

"Okay, you've talked me down . . . for you only fifteen dollars."

"Give me water."

"You drive a hard bargain, but ten dollars is my final offer."

"I need water."

"I see; well, I guess we won't be doing business together. Tell you what; just crawl up there over the sand dune and you'll see a nightclub."

Will summons all his strength and crawls over the sand dune and reaches the door of the nightclub. The doorman is standing out in front and stops Will from entering.

"Hey, buddy, can't you read? All customers must wear ties."

Belva, a rich old widow, marries a young gigolo, and they spend their summer honeymoon at Lake Tahoe. When they get back, one of the woman's friends is asking her how things went.

"It was wonderful," Belva says, "he loves me so much. He's actually trying to get me into better shape."

"How's that?" asks the friend.

"Well, every morning on our honeymoon, he'd take me swimming. He'd row me out to the middle of the lake and I'd swim back."

"That's a pretty long swim for a woman your age."

"Not really. The hard part was getting out of the sack."

Sam is on his deathbed; his wife of fifty years is sitting close by.

"Rose, I've been thinking," says the dying man. "When our first house burned down, you were at my side. And it was you, Rose, who was there when the car broke down on the interstate. Rose, you were the one who was there when the business went under and I lost everything. Now I am dying and it's you, Rose, who is at my side."

"Yes, Sam."

"I tell you one thing, Rose," he says. "You've been a real jinx."

Floyd, an eighty-year-old man, is sitting at a bar and in walks a gorgeous young Swedish flight attendant. She's the most beautiful woman he's ever seen. He offers to buy her a drink and they start talking. One thing leads to another and the old man takes her home with him.

The next day the old man is passing a Catholic church and he goes into the confessional. "Father," Floyd says, "last night I slept with a twenty-year-old stewardess and we had sex."

The priest says, "The flesh is weak, but you have God's forgiveness. Say three Hail Marys."

"But, Father, I'm not Catholic."

"Then why did you come to Confession and tell me this?"

"Father, I'm telling everybody."

Joe is on his deathbed and he says to his wife, "When I die, will you marry someone else?"

"No, darling," cries his Marsha, "I will be faithful to your memory for the rest of my life."

"No"—Joe sighs—"you are still young, it's only right that you marry again."

"If it makes you happy," she says.

"If you remarry," says the dying man, "would you give the guy my new car?"

"Of course not," says the wife. "I'd never let him use your car. That car is your pride and joy."

"It's only right that he should drive my car," says Joe.

"If you insist," says Marsha, "he'll get your car."

"And my golf clubs," says the dying husband, "would you give him my clubs?"

"No," says his wife, "he's left-handed."

John is talking to the bartender. "You know," says John, "I have this problem, I just can't get enough sex. I have sex with different women three times a day. It's driving me crazy. I don't know what to do."

"I saw something like this on a talk show," says the bartender.

"What did they say?" asks John.

"They said that some form of relaxation can help. Try yoga," suggests the bartender.

Three weeks pass and John comes into the bar again and the bartender says, "Say, how's it going?"

"I'm doing yoga," says John.

"Does it help?" asks the bartender.

"It sure does," says John. "Now I can have sex standing on my head."

Alice goes to a fortune-teller and has her palm read. The fortune-teller looks at the woman's hand, shakes her head, and says, "Prepare yourself for widowhood . . . your husband will die violently."

"I just have one question," says Alice. "Will I get acquitted?"

It's Saturday at noon and a guy sticks his head inside a barbershop and says to the barber, "How long you going to be?"

The barber looks at the full waiting room and says, "At least an hour and a half." The guy nods, leaves, and never comes back.

The next Saturday the same guy comes by the barbershop at noon, sticks his head in, and says to the barber, "How long are you going to be?" Again the barber tells him an hour or two. The guy disappears . . . until the next Saturday. This happens every Saturday for a month.

Finally, the barber can't stand it any longer. He tells his buddy, "At noon today a guy is going to stick his head in my shop and ask me how long I'm going to be, then he's going to walk away. Do me a favor, follow him and let me know where he goes."

His buddy agrees. The guy shows up at noon and does his usual thing. An hour later, the friend shows up to report to the barber.

"Did you follow him?" asks the barber.

"Yeah," says his friend.

"Well, where did he go?" asks the barber.

"To your house."

Betty is sitting in a bar, showing off her diamond engagement ring to her friend. "This is one of the largest diamonds in the world. It's called the Schwartz Diamond. But, of course, it comes with a curse," she says.

"Wow," says her friend. "What's the curse?"

"Seymour Schwartz."

It's early Monday morning and the owner is just opening his drugstore. A guy runs in and slams a package down on the counter.

"I came in here Friday night and got twelve dozen condoms," he screams at the druggist. "I counted them and there's only eleven dozen here!"

The druggist looks at the man and says, "Sorry I ruined your weekend."

The judge says to the little old lady, "I understand you want a divorce. On what grounds?"

"We have about two acres, Your Honor."

"No, no. I mean do you have a grudge?" asks the judge.

"Of course we do. It's attached to the house and fits two cars."

"You don't understand," says the judge. "Is there a problem; for example, does he beat you up?"

"Only if the alarm clock is on his side of the bed," answers the woman.

"I'm sorry," says the judge, "I just don't understand why you want a divorce."

"Because he just doesn't understand me."

A spaceship lands near a bar. The aliens go inside and kidnap a man and woman and take them on board. The aliens tell the humans that no harm will come to them if they just mate so they can observe the procedure.

When the humans finish, one of the spacemen asks, "How long does it take for a new baby earth creature to be born?"

"Nine months," says the woman.

"Oh," says the alien. "Then why were you in such a hurry at the end?"

Kevin and his wife are at a party. A beautiful young woman is playing the piano and Kevin spends the whole evening hanging around the piano, talking to her and ignoring his wife. He's leaning against the piano talking to the woman when he loses his balance and the cover of the piano comes slamming down on his fingers.

Kevin and his wife are driving home and his wife says, "Remind me to get a cold steak to put on your black eye when we get home."

"But it's my fingers that hurt," says Kevin.

"We're not home yet!"

A doctor and his wife are having a drink in a cocktail lounge when a woman in a low-cut dress, spike heels, and wearing lots of makeup comes over and whispers something into the doctor's ear. The wife gives the doctor an icy stare and the doctor says, "I know her professionally."

"Oh," says his wife, "yours or hers?"

Jack walks into Smitty's Bar and says, "Want to go for a spin in my new car?"

"You have a new car?" says Smitty. "How the hell did you get a new car?"

"Well," says Jack, "the other night I was in here and I met this woman. She takes me for a ride in her new car and I kissed her a few times and she told me I could have anything I wanted."

"So?"

"I took her car."

Smitty hires Joyce, a beautiful woman, to tend bar. She is working her first night and two male customers, one at either end of the bar, keep asking her to go out. Joyce wants nothing to do with either one of them. Toward the end of the night, one guy slips her a piece of paper with his address written on it and his house key. She takes the paper and the key and whispers to the guy, "Get into bed, turn out all the lights, and I'll be there at midnight."

Then she goes to the other end of the bar and hands the paper and the key to the other guy and says, "Meet me here at midnight. I'll be in bed with the lights out."

Ruth is talking to a marriage counselor. "My husband is having an affair with another woman," she says.

"And this disturbs you?" asks the counselor.

"Yes, it really bothers me," says Ruth.

"And you've come to me for advice on how to break it up?"

"Oh, no!" says Ruth. "I was hoping you could tell me what the other woman sees in him."

In the Ozarks, a man is being attacked by a giant grizzly bear. The man's wife is sitting on a tree stump with a rifle over her knees, watching the bear claw at the man and rip his limbs off.

A neighbor yells, "Why don't you shoot the beast?"

"I was hoping the bear would spare me the trouble."

A Martian lands in the middle of Manhattan. He's standing next to a traffic signal that's blinking ... walk ... don't walk ... walk ... don't walk.

"Baby, I love you," says the Martian, "but you gotta stop being such a nag."

Pam has been in psychoanalysis for six years. She decides that it is time to end her therapy.

"Doctor," Pam says, "I've known you for six years. May I kiss you good-bye?"

"That's not possible," says the doctor. "Why, I shouldn't even be here on the couch with you."

Tim goes to Confession and he says to the priest, "Father, I have sinned. I am not married and I had sex with a woman six times last night."

"This is a terrible sin, my son; in order to forgive you, I must have more details. Tell me who was this woman ... was it Bridget O'Flaherty?"

"Oh, no, Father, it wasn't Bridget."

"Was it Margaret Mary O'Malley?"

"No, Father, it wasn't Margaret Mary."

"Well then, was it Rosie O'Mara?"

"No, Father."

"I cannot give you forgiveness unless you tell me her name," says the priest.

Tim is leaving the church and he runs into his friend Pete.

"So did the priest forgive you?" asks Pete.

"No," says Tim, "but I got a great list of names."

A ninety-five-year-old woman wanders into a bar early one Sunday afternoon. "Excuse me, sir," she says in a timid voice. "May I trade in this old coin for a new one?"

"Certainly," says the bartender. "My grandmother is the same way, she always wants a shiny new quarter for the collection basket."

"Well, it's not for church," answers the old lady with a blush. "You see, if the quarter is bent like this, it tends to jam the condom machine."

Karen is in a singles bar and is having no luck meeting a man. A sad-looking guy sits down next to her and orders a drink. They start talking and the guy tells her that he just got out of prison.

"What were you in for?" she asks.

"I was in for twenty years. I hit my wife with a golf club, put her body in the trunk of my car, and threw her in the river. Three days later, her body washed ashore and I got caught."

"Oh, good," says Karen, "so you're single."

4

GOOD SPORTS

Every bar has its weekend warriors. They come in many forms, from softball players to bowlers to golfers.... they play hard and they laugh hard, even when the joke is on them.

Billy, a Chicago bar owner, makes arrangements to fly to San Francisco for the first Bears games of the season. There's a group of friends from his tavern making the trip with him. He is sitting on the plane and he happens to notice an empty seat in the row in front of him. Knowing that the flight is sold out, he leans over and says, "Excuse me, lady, I don't mean to be rude, but do you know why this seat is empty?"

"Well," says the lady. "My husband and I have been Bears fans all our lives and we have never missed a game, no matter where they play. Unfortunately, he died."

"I am so sorry to hear that," says Billy, "but don't you have any friends who might have gone with you?"

"Yes," she says, "but they're all at the funeral."

Tom is stranded on a desert island for twenty years. One day he's strolling along the beach and a beautiful woman appears out of the surf wearing a wet suit. She walks toward him and waves.

"Hi," she says. "How would you like a nice cold beer?" And with that, she unzips her wet suit, revealing her stunning figure, and she pulls out a cold can of beer.

"This is great," says Tom. "I haven't had a beer in twenty years."

"And I bet you'd like a cigarette, too." And the well-endowed woman unzips her wet suit and pulls out a pack of cigarettes and a lighter.

"How did you know?" asks Tom. "I've been dying for a smoke."

"Now," says the beautiful woman, "how would you like to play around?" Once more, she starts to unzip her wet suit.

"Unbelievable," says the man, "you've got golf clubs in there, too?"

Shirley, Sally, and Dorothy play bridge each Wednesday at Alma's house. While she is shuffling the cards Alma says, "Listen, gals, when you use the bathroom upstairs, I have a little surprise for you."

Shirley excuses herself and goes to the bathroom. A few minutes later, she comes downstairs and says, "You won't believe it! When I sat down, it played a Strauss waltz."

After playing a few hands, Sally feels the call of nature and she hurries to the second floor. She returns humming and says, "I sat down and it played 'Moon River.'"

Finally, it is Dorothy's turn. Ten minutes pass, then fifteen; finally, after half an hour, Alma gets worried and goes upstairs. There is Dorothy on the floor, wiping it up.

"What happened?" asks Alma.

"Wouldn't you know it?" says Dorothy. "When I sat down, it played 'The Star-Spangled Banner'!"

It is the last game of the year. Tim has sat on the bench all season. It looks like he isn't going to play at all. Tim's team is losing by one point with one minute left to play. The coach turns to Tim and says, "We can't stop the clock ... we've run out of time-outs ... get in there and get hurt."

Mike is bored and decides to take up a hobby. He goes shopping with his wife and buys a jigsaw puzzle in a hobby shop. Months go by and his wife asks him how the puzzle is progressing.

"Great," says Mike. "I put together six pieces already."

"Six pieces? That's all you've done in three months. A little slow, aren't you?"

"No, look at the box. It says from three to five years."

Paul and his minister are playing golf at their local country club. Paul can't hit the ball, and when he does, it lands in the rough. Each time he swings at the ball, he says, "Oh, shit!"

After many "Oh, shits!" the minister says, "You have to watch your language. God will punish you."

But a few minutes later, he drives his ball into the sand trap and yells, "Oh, shit!"

A hand reaches out of a huge cloud and thrusts down a huge bolt of lightning, which hits the minister. A deep voice comes out of the cloud and says, "Oh, shit!"

Night is falling; a man is out hiking by himself when he loses his footing and falls off a cliff. He manages to grab hold of a small tree and is hanging over a yawning chasm with nothing but blackness below. He shouts, "Is anybody down there?"

"I am down here," says a great voice, "let go of the tree. You can trust Me, I am God!"

There is a long silence and then the hiker shouts, "Is anybody else down there?"

Pete comes home from the country club, throws his clubs into the closet, and flops down on the couch, exhausted. "What's the matter, honey? You look so tired," says his wife, Gayle.

"I had the worst day. I was playing in a twosome with Bill and he drops dead while he is putting on the tenth hole," says Pete.

"Oh, my God, how awful," says Gayle.

"You're not kidding," says Pete. "For the last eight holes, it was drive the ball, drag Bill . . . drive the ball, drag Bill . . . drive the ball. . . ."

Grant talks about nothing but golf, day in and day out. He is driving his wife crazy—all he talks about is putts, sand traps, birdies, and eagles.

Finally, one morning at breakfast, she reaches the breaking point. "Listen," she says, "I can't take it anymore, all you talk about is golf. I don't want to hear about it anymore. Just once I'd like to have a meal where you aren't talking about golf."

Grant looks at his wife and asks, "What do I talk about?"

"What difference does it make?" snaps his wife. "Talk about sex."

"All right," says Grant. "Gosh, I wonder who my caddie is screwing?"

Bill, the golf pro, walks into the clubhouse and orders a drink from the bartender. "I've had the worst day," he confesses. "I just played a round with Jim Burns."

"Has his game improved any?" asks the bartender.

"He beat me," says the pro.

"But he's never beat anyone, how could he beat you?"

"We were on the first tee and he asks, 'Do I get a handicap?'

"I say, 'Sure, anything you want!'

"And he says, 'I want two gotchas!'

"And of course, I say, 'What's a gotcha?'

"And Jim says, 'You'll find out.'

"Jim takes his first swing and the ball goes about fifty feet or so. I take my turn, and just as I am about to hit the ball he grabs my privates and says, 'Gotcha.' Of course I miss the ball completely."

The bartender says, "But that was only one stroke and he only had one gotcha left."

"Have you ever tried to swing at a golf ball waiting for that second gotcha?"

An all-male crew is rowing their boat on the river, training for the Olympics. A motorboat roars by, upsets their boat, and all the men are thrown into the river. They swim ashore and take off their wet clothes to dry themselves. They are standing on the shore totally nude when a boatful of school-teachers from the local school comes floating by. All the men wrap their jerseys around their loins— all but one guy, who wraps his jersey around his head and face.

After the boat goes by, one of the men turns to

the guy and says, "What the hell did you do that for?"

"Well," he says, "I don't know about you, but the people I know usually recognize each other by their faces."

"So what's your handicap?"

"I'm a scratch golfer. I write down all my good scores and I scratch out all my bad scores."

A priest and a rabbi are enjoying a friendly game of chess when the priest says, "Tell me, rabbi, have you ever tasted ham?"

The rabbi blushes. "To tell you the truth, I have. I was in college. I was eating a sandwich and I thought it was corned beef, but wouldn't you know—it was ham. But now it's your turn, Father. Tell me—have you ever been with a woman?"

"I have to be honest; before I entered the priesthood, I had a few dates with a woman."

The rabbi smiles and says, "It's better than ham, isn't it?"

Roger goes to Caesar's Palace in Las Vegas every night and asks the guests for money. He goes up to everyone in the casino and says, "If you give me a hundred dollars, I'll double your money in no time and pay you right back!"

Night after night, people just ignore him and walk away.

One night his luck changes and he runs into a rich Texan, who gives him a crisp hundred-dollar bill and says, "Here you are, have fun."

Roger thanks the man, goes over to the blackjack table, and loses the money in five minutes.

The next night he sees the rich Texan again and

asks him for some money. Again the Texan gives him a hundred-dollar bill and just as quickly Roger gambles it away.

The same scenario is repeated every night for three weeks. Every night the Texan gives him money and every night he gambles it away.

Finally, totally frustrated, Roger tells one of his friends about his experience with the rich Texan. And the guy says to him, "Dump the Texan, he's bad luck for you!"

Two elderly gentlemen are spending the afternoon at the racetrack. One of the men is a seasoned veteran at the track and the other is there for the first time. They are studying the racing form and the inexperienced man says, "Which horse do I bet on?"

"I've got a system that never fails," says the skilled player. "How many children do you have?"

"Three."

"Then bet on number three."

Sure enough, number three crosses the finish line first and the elderly man collects his winnings.

When it is time for the second race, he says, "Now which horse do I bet on?"

"Do you have any grandchildren?"

"I am proud to say I have five lovely grandchildren."

"Good, bet half your winnings on horse number five."

Number five gets off to a shaky start, but as the horses go into the last quarter mile he overtakes the pack and wins the race by a nose. Now the inexperienced man is really starting to enjoy himself.

"This is unbelievable; now what should I bet on?"

"In the past year, how often have you and your wife been intimate?"

"Let's see, this is October. There was that trip to the Grand Canyon ... and my birthday ... all together, I'd say seven ... yes, exactly seven times this year."

"Bet it all on number seven."

Horse number one wins.

"Damn," says the disappointed loser. "I shouldn't have lied."

It is just about dusk and three guys are mountain climbing. They are making their way up the steep side of a mountain when one of them loses his footing, falls about fifty feet, and lands on a ledge below. The other two yell down at him, "Bill, are you okay?"

"I'm down here," Bill answers. "I think I broke both my arms!"

"We'll toss down a rope and pull you up."

In no time flat, they are hoisting Bill up on the end of the rope. They are tugging and grunting, working in unison to bring their friend up to safety. When he is about halfway up, one of the men remembers that Bill said he broke both his arms.

He yells, "Bill, if you broke both your arms, how are you holding on?"

Bill says, "With my *TEEEEEEEEEEETH* ..."

Bob, an insurance salesman, takes his wife to the state fair. The wife is riding on the ferris wheel when the chair she is sitting in suddenly breaks free from the struts. She is hanging upside down on the ferris wheel, clutching one of the spokes. A large crowd gathers and watches the woman's plight in horror.

The insurance salesman looks up and shouts, "Honey! Honey! Throw out some of our business cards!"

A man from San Francisco, a man from New York, and a man from Chicago are granted an interview with God. They all get to ask him one question. The man from San Francisco asks, "God, will there ever come a time when we have no more earthquakes?"

"Yes," God answers, "but not in your lifetime."

Then the New Yorker gets to ask a question. "God, will there ever come a time when there will be no crime in the streets?"

"Yes," replies God, "but not in your lifetime."

Finally, it is time for the man from Chicago to ask his question. "God, will the Cubs ever win the World Series?"

"Yes," says God, "but not in *my* lifetime."

Jim is playing a game of golf. He is on the eighteenth hole and he only has two balls left, an old one and a brand-new one. The shot has to pass over a man-made lake and he is wondering which ball to play.

Jim stands there trying to decide when the clouds part and a booming voice says, "Have faith. Play ... the ... new ... ball!"

Jim can't believe his ears, but he tees up the new ball and is about to hit it when again the clouds part. The heavenly voice says, "Take ... a ... practice ... swing."

Practice swing? But what can he do—he follows the divine advice and takes a practice swing.

Filled with confidence, he is just about to hit the

ball for real when the clouds part a third time and the voice calls out, "Play . . . the . . . old . . . ball!"

A gambler walks up to a craps table in Reno. He takes the dice and lays down a five-thousand-dollar bet. He blows on the dice, shakes them, and throws them on the table. As he does so a third cube falls from his sleeve and lands on the table next to the other two.

The house operator doesn't blink. He picks up the two dice and puts the third cube into his pocket. As he hands them back to the gambler he says, "Roll again, your point is sixteen."

Two men are talking about where their sons are going to college. "My son is trying to decide between Georgia Tech and Miami University," one of them says.

"Don't let him go to Georgia," says the other man. "They only have two kinds of students: football players and woman that are uglier than dog meat!"

"My wife graduated from Georgia Tech," yells the first man.

"Really? What position did she play?"

A bloodied fighter is lying in the boxing ring. The referee starts the count. "One, two, three, four . . ."

The downed boxer's manager shouts to him, "Don't get up until eight."

"No problem," says the fighter. "What time is it now?"

Mike, a tavern owner who loves to gamble, gets himself hopelessly in debt. Three local bookies are out to get him. Desperate to get out of this messy situation, Mike decides to notify the newspapers that he has committed suicide. He plans to stage a mock funeral and convince the three thugs he is dead.

The bar closes down in his memory; many of the customers send flowers and lots of friends are mourning the loss of a good buddy. Everyone is filing past the coffin, paying their last respects.

Then it is the three bookies' turn.

The first bookie says, "Well, Mike, you went out owing me a bundle, but I'll miss you."

"Bye, pal," says the second bookie, "it was fun knowing you."

The third bookie is enraged. "You rat," he screams. "You had to go and die when you owe me ten thousand dollars. I know you're dead, but I don't care; I'm going to do this anyway." He pulls a revolver from his jacket and aims it at the supposedly dead man's heart.

"Relax," shrieks the corpse as he sits up. "You I'll pay."

A trainer enters a six-year-old horse in a race. The horse has no previous record, so the odds are 90 to 1 against him. When the race begins, the horse takes off like a rocket. He wins by ten lengths. The racing officials are a bit suspicious and call the owner in for questioning.

"How come this horse has never raced before?" they ask. "You've had him for six years."

"To tell you the truth, we couldn't catch him until he was five."

An elderly couple is playing shuffleboard on a luxury liner. Suddenly the captain announces from the bridge, "Ladies and gentlemen, our ship is sinking . . . does anyone know how to pray?"

The old man steps forward and says, "I know how to pray, Captain."

"That's great. You pray and the rest of us will put on life jackets. We're one short."

At the racetrack, a guy makes several trips to the window and places his money on Mr. New Shoes to win the last race. On his third trip to the window, a stranger steps up to him. "Excuse me," says the stranger. "It's not really any of my business, but if I were you, I wouldn't bet all my money on Mr. New Shoes. He's not going to win."

"How do you know?" asks the man.

"Don't tell anyone, but I own Mr. New Shoes, and believe me, he's not going to win."

"Well, it's going to be a slow race, 'cause I own the other four horses."

Max and Ernie are playing racquetball at the local gym. As they are changing clothes in the locker room Max takes off his T-shirt and shorts. He is wearing a bra and a lace garter belt.

"My God," says Ernie, "when did you start wearing women's underwear?"

"Ever since my wife found them in my glove compartment."

Smitty the bartender comes back after his two-week vacation, tanned and rested.

"Say, Smitty, where did you go?" asks one of his customers.

"Actually, a friend of mine invited me up to his cabin. Two weeks in the mountains, no nightlife, no parties, and not a woman within miles!" answers Smitty.

"Was it fun?"

"Who went?" says Smitty.

Jack is playing golf in a foursome. It's his turn to play, so he tees off. He watches as the ball veers off to the right over the tops of the trees and onto the street. He hears a terrible crash. He's so upset he throws down his driver and runs back to the clubhouse. There, he discovers that his golf ball hit the windshield of a car and the driver of the car lost control and ran into a telephone pole. "Oh, my God," cries Jack, "this is awful! What am I going to do?"

One of his foursome walks over to him, puts his hand on his shoulder, and says, "If you just put your fingers like this and tighten up a little on your grip . . ."

A chartered bus breaks down in front of a tavern and a professional basketball team files into the bar. The waitress is having a difficult time wending her way through the sea of seven-foot-tall men. As she takes an order from one of the men she can't help noticing that he is only four-one.

"Are you one of the coaches?" she asks the tiny man.

"No," he answers, "I am a player."

"I don't mean to be rude," says the shocked waitress, "but aren't you a little short to be playing pro basketball?"

"Shh," he says, "I lied about my height."

A spaceship lands in Las Vegas and a Martian is taking a tour of the gambling casinos. He is watching as one person after another pumps the arm of a slot machine. Finally, he walks over to the slot machine and says, "I don't know what office you're running for, buddy, but when you're shaking hands, try and smile a little more."

Ned is down on his luck in Las Vegas. He has gambled away all his money and has to borrow a dime from another gambler just to use the men's room. The stall happens to be open and he uses the dime in a slot machine and hits the jackpot. He takes his winnings and goes to the blackjack table and turns his small winnings into a million dollars.

Wealthy beyond his wildest dreams, Ned goes on the lecture circuit, where he tells his incredible story. He tells his audiences that he is eternally grateful to his benefactor, and if he ever finds the man, he will share his fortune with him. After months of speaking, a man in the audience jumps up and says, "I am that man. I was the one who gave you the dime."

"You aren't the one I'm looking for. I mean the guy who left the door open!"

A golfer tees up his ball and says to his playing partner, "This one's good for one long drive and a putt." He swings and tears up the course; the ball lifts into the air and goes all of four feet.

His partner shakes his head and says, "That's going to be one hell of a putt."

A few of the guys have a weekly poker game; they play in the back room of the bar. They are always bugged by one of the patrons who loves to kibitz. Tonight, when they sit down to play, the kibitzer is nowhere in sight. "I know," says one of the players. "When he shows up, let's make up a game that no one ever heard of, then he'll have to shut up."

The kibitzer makes his appearance and the game begins. The dealer gives every other man a card, then tosses the rest of the deck into the middle of the table and says, "A whammy! I'll pass."

The man on his right says, "I have a ziggle, I'll bet a dollar."

The next man says, "I'll raise you a dollar, 'cause I have a fratsel."

The third man says, "Hmm, I've got a zoup. I'll see you and raise you two."

The kibitzer says, "Are you nuts! You can't beat a ziggle and a fratsel with a lousy zoup!"

A football fan is at his first game of the season. He leaves his seat to get a couple of hot dogs. When he returns, he leans over and asks a woman who is seated on the aisle, "Did I step on your feet when I went out?"

"Yes, you did," says the woman, ready to accept his apology.

"Good," he says, "now I know I'm in the right row."

Pete and Tom have bowled together every day since they retired twenty years ago. One day they are putting on their bowling shoes and they get into a discussion about whether there will be bowling alleys in heaven. They make a pact that the first one to die will come back and visit the other one. Pete dies first, and true to their pact, he pays a visit to Tom.

"What's heaven like?" asks Tom. "Do they have bowling?"

"I have good news and bad news about that. The good news is we have bowling like you've never seen. We play twenty-four hours a day. In fact, we are choosing up teams for next week's tournament right now."

"Sounds great! But what's the bad news?"

"You're on my team."

Two guys are out fishing in the middle of a lake in a secluded spot in the Rockies. One hour goes by, two hours go by, and neither of them gets so much as a nibble. Finally, the first guy says, "I caught a five-pound trout out here last week."

Another hour passes and the first guy says, "Beautiful day."

Two more hours pass, and the first guy says, "Looks like it might rain."

"Look," says the second guy, "did you come out here to talk or to fish?"

A golfer dies and goes to hell. He's amazed when Satan gives him a tour. As far as the eye can see, there are acres and acres of rolling green golf courses, each more beautiful than the last. The devil hands him a golf bag with a custom-made set of golf clubs.

"Unbelievable," says the man, "where can I get some golf balls?"

"Don't have any," Satan says, laughing, "that's the hell of it."

After a horse race, the trainer is talking to the jockey.

"There was a big gap between the leaders at the three-quarter mile post. Why didn't you move up into it?"

"The gap was moving faster than the horse."

Two guys are duck hunting for the first time. They are out in the blind for hours and are having no luck at all. Finally, one guy turns to the other and says, "Hey, do you think we're throwing the dogs high enough?"

Bart and his wife are out golfing when Bart slices the ball and it ends up in a cow pasture. He finds the ball near a barn that's blocking him from the green. His wife says, "I've got an idea. Why don't I open the doors on either end and you can drive the ball right through the barn?"

Bart figures he has nothing to lose. His wife opens the doors and he swings at the ball. Unfortunately, Bart misses the doors and the ball hits his wife in the head, killing her instantly.

Six months later, he's playing the same golf course and he tees off on the same hole and his ball again ends up in the cow pasture. His golf partner says, "I've got an idea. I can open the barn doors and you can hit it through!"

Bart leans on his golf club and says, "No way! Last time I tried that, I ended up taking a nine."

Every night before he goes to sleep, Jeff gets down on his knees and says, "God, please, please let me win the lottery."

Jeff repeats the same thing every night for months and nothing ever happens. Finally, he hears a voice from the heavens.

"God, God is that You?"

"Yes, my son, it is."

"God, why haven't I won the lottery?"

"You have to do something before you can win."

"What, God? I'll do anything."

"First," says God, "you have to buy a ticket."

William is getting a physical and the doctor notices that his shins are covered with bruises.

"You either play soccer or hockey," observes the doctor.

"No," says the man. "My wife and I play bridge."

Jerry is just about to tee off on the first hole when a woman in a wedding dress comes running toward him. She takes a golf club and starts chasing him around the green.

"I told you," he yells, "only if it rains."

Bill is sitting at home watching a football game when the phone rings. "You gotta get over here right away; it's an emergency," says Jim when Bill picks up the receiver.

"But it's almost the end of the fourth quarter and the score is tied," says Bill.

"I don't care, this is an emergency! Get over here right away and bring me a couple of beers."

Bill grabs a few beers from the refrigerator, gets in his car, and drives over to Jim's house. He finds Jim sitting in front of the television set watching the highlights of the football game.

"You made me miss the end of the game. What's the big emergency?"

"It *is* an emergency! I don't get paid until tomorrow and I ran out of beer."

Stan is fishing and is having no luck at all. He walks a little way downstream and finds a net strung across the creek that's filled with trout. He is stuffing the fish into his basket when the game warden spots him.

"Hey, buddy, you're under arrest for having too many fish."

"Thank God," says the man. "For a minute there, I thought you were the guy that owns the net."

A guy is out duck hunting when the game warden asks to see his license. "Hey, you can't be out here hunting with last year's license," says the game warden to the man.

"Don't worry," says the hunter, "I'm only shooting at the ducks I missed last year."

A new golfer is out for his first time on the course. Bud is showing him how to play the game; he hits the ball off the first tee and it lands in a deep rut. He hacks it out there and the ball rolls into a sand trap. After four strokes, the ball goes into a gopher hole and then lands in a puddle. Finally, Bud putts the ball into the cup.

His friend says to Bud, "Let's see you hit it out of there."

A doctor and his friend go deep-sea fishing. After a few hours out in the boat, they catch a swordfish. When they get to shore, they want to weigh the giant fish but can't find a scale. The doctor says, "I've got an idea; let's take him to my office and we can weigh him on one of my scales."

The doctor has the fish's tail and his friend is holding the fish around the head. They manage to get it in the backdoor of the office and weigh it. Leaving the office, they lug the big fish past the patients in the waiting room. Not missing a beat, the doctor says in a loud voice, "If he's not feeling any better, bring him back tomorrow."

Greg and Harry get into an argument while they're fishing off a bridge. Greg says, "I bet I'll catch the first fish."

"Bet you don't," says Harry.

Just then Greg loses his footing and falls into the river. Harry yells down to him, "If you're going to dive for them, the bet is off."

Two golfers are just about to tee off. One guy says to the other, "Hey, there's my lawyer in the clubhouse."

"Don't be silly," says the other guy, "you can't hit him from here."

A farmer gets tired of having his animals shot at during hunting season, so he comes up with a plan. He paints the names of his animals on their sides. He paints P-I-G on his prize sow. His Jersey has C-O-W painted on her side. He does the same for all his large farm animals.

The next day a group of hunters are hunting near his farm. One of the hunters spots something behind a bush and yells, "Deer!" A flurry of gunshots rings out. When they look behind the bush, they discover a tractor riddled with gunshots that is labeled "John Deere."

Two guys are sitting at a bar; one turns to the other and says, "What do you think of the Indianapolis 500?"

"They're innocent!"

A fisherman is out in a boat all day and doesn't even have a nibble. Just as he's rowing his boat back to shore a fish leaps out of the water and lands in his boat. The guys picks up the fish and tosses it back into the water and yells, "If you ain't gonna bite, you ain't gonna ride."

Robert is walking by his church and the minister spots him and says, "I know that you didn't come to services last Sunday so you could play golf."

Robert says, "Minister, that's a lie! And I've got the fish to prove it."

Hennessey is at the track when he spots Father Ryan making the sign of the cross over one of the horses. He takes this as a sign from God and bets all his money on the horse. The horse finishes last.

Hennessey finds Father Ryan and says, "Father, I saw you blessing that horse, so I put all my money on him."

"I wasn't blessing him," says the priest. "I was giving him last rites."

An old man is fishing in a canoe in the middle of a peaceful lake. Out of nowhere a speedboat pulls up and the wave action nearly knocks the canoe over. The guy in the boat turns on his radio full blast and dumps an empty can into the lake. He drops his line into the water; it gets tangled in the old man's line. He's trying to free his fishing line and he falls into the lake.

"Help! Help!" he yells. "I can't swim."

"Neither can I ," says the old man, "but I don't make such a fuss about it."

A couple of hikers are walking in the woods when they come face-to-face with a giant bear. The grizzly stands over seven feet tall on his hind legs; he is snarling at the hikers.

One of the hikers slowly puts his knapsack down and starts putting on his sneakers.

"What the hell are you doing?" whispers the other guy. "Don't you know he can run over fifty miles an hour. What good will your sneakers do? How the hell are you going to outrun a bear?"

"Well," says the guy, "I don't have to outrun the bear. I just have to outrun you."

Jim walks into a bar and says, "I just bowled a terrific game. It's the closest I've ever come to a perfect 300."

"What was your score?" asks the bartender.

"Fifty-eight!"

"Hey, Bill, how come you catch so many fish?"

"I have a system," says Bill.

"What's that?"

"When I wake up in the morning, if my wife is sleeping on her left side, then I fish off the left side of the boat. But if I wake up and she's sleeping on her right side, I'll fish from the right side of the boat."

"What if she's sleeping on her back?"

"Then I don't go fishing."

Ted dies and goes to hell. Satan greets him at the entrance and asks him if he wants to go to regular hell or football lover's hell.

"In each place," explains the devil, "you are frequently doused with gasoline and set on fire."

"So what's the difference?"

"Take football lover's hell," says Satan. "They're usually so busy talking about last week's game they forget to bring the matches."

5

BARTENDER CLASSICS

No one can tell a funny story like a bartender. Take a few moments while we share our premium stock of jokes guaranteed to hoist your spirits.

The sales manager of a large company is complaining to his assistant about one of his salesmen. "Bill is so forgetful, it's amazing to me that he can sell anything. He never remembers a thing I tell him. I asked him to pick me up a sandwich on the way back from lunch and he's so scattered I'm not sure he'll remember to come back."

Just then his office door bursts open and Bill rushes in. He says, "Boss, you'll never guess what happened! I was eating my lunch at the deli down the street and I saw Bob Smith. He hasn't bought anything from us in years. Well, we were having lunch together and by the time it was over he gave me an order for two million dollars!"

The sales manager turns to his assistant and says, "What did I tell you, he forgot my sandwich."

A wealthy man is taking a group of journalists on a tour of his new mansion. In the back of his property, he has the largest swimming pool any of them has ever seen. However, the huge pool is filled with alligators. The rich man tells the writers, "I think that a man should be measured by his courage. Courage is what made me a wealthy man. In fact, I will offer you a challenge; if anyone is brave enough to dive into this pool, and swims through those alligators and makes it to the other side, I will give that person anything they desire! You can have my house, my cars, my money, just name it."

Everyone laughs at the outrageous offer and proceeds to follow the man on the tour of his vast estate. Suddenly they hear a loud splash. Everyone looks around and sees one of the journalists in the pool swimming for his life. He dodges the alligators left and right and makes it to the edge of the pool and pulls himself out just as a huge 'gator is about to snap off his leg.

The wealthy man approaches the man and says, "You are amazing. I've never seen anything like that. You are a true man of courage; tell me what you want. Anything of mine is yours."

The man, panting for breath, looks up and says, "I just want to know one thing. Who the hell pushed me in the pool?"

Bruce is anxious to sell the office manager of a larger firm his computer system. If he convinces the office manager to convert to his system, it will mean several thousand dollars in commissions for him. Bruce tries to bribe the office manager with a free home computer.

"Oh, my conscience wouldn't let me take a gift," says the manager.

"I can understand that," says Bruce. "I tell you what. I'll sell it to you for a dollar."

"In that case," answers the manager, "I'll take two!"

Juan comes up to the Mexican border on his bicycle. He's got two large bags over his shoulders. The guard stops him and says, "What's in the bags?"

"Sand," answers Juan.

The guard says, "We'll just see about that—get off the bike."

The guard takes the bags and rips them apart; he empties them out and finds nothing in them but sand. He detains Juan overnight and has the sand analyzed, only to discover that there is nothing but pure sand in the bags. The guard releases Juan, puts the sand into new bags, hefts them onto the man's shoulders, and lets him cross the border.

A week later, the same thing happens. The guard asks, "What have you got?"

"Sand," says Juan.

The guard does his thorough examination and discovers that the bags contain nothing but sand. He puts the sand back into the bags then onto Juan's shoulders. Juan crosses the border on his bicycle.

This sequence of events is repeated every day for three years. Finally, Juan doesn't show up one day and the guard meets him in a cantina in Mexico.

"Hey, buddy," says the guard, "I know you are smuggling something. It's driving me crazy. It's all I think about; I can't sleep. Just between you and me, what are you smuggling?"

Juan sips his beer and says, "Bicycles."

Jim the bartender always shows up for work at exactly five o'clock. He is never late. One day five o'clock comes and goes and Jim is nowhere to be seen. The bar manager looks at his watch and begins muttering to himself. Finally, at six, Jim shows up. His face is all bruised, his clothes are ripped and torn, his glasses are bent. He limps to the time clock and punches in, and then he puts on an apron and hobbles to the bar. He says, "I fell and rolled down two flights of stairs in my apartment building. I nearly killed myself."

The bar manager says, "Rolling down two flights of stairs took you an hour?"

An army general is standing in front of a telephone booth without the correct change. He flags down a passing private and says, "Have you got change for a dollar?"

"I think I do," says the private. "Let me check."

The general is offended; he draws himself up and says, "Is that any way to address a general? Let's just do this again. Do you have change for a dollar?"

The private salutes smartly and says, "No, sir."

A guy goes to a tailor because he wants a new suit. The salesman takes out a long form and asks him his name, his age, his religion, his occupation, his political party, his astrological sign, where his mother and father were born. . . .

"Why all these questions?" asks the customer. "I just want to buy a suit."

"Well," says the salesman, "this is not a run-of-the-mill tailor shop. Each suit is as individual as the person wearing it. We make a study of your likes and dislikes, your personality profile, and your background. Then we send all this information to our buyers around the world. Wool from Scotland, the finest cashmere from England. We have buyers in South America and as far away as

New Zealand. We want the fabric to be just right for you and you alone.

"After we get the material, we have our customers go through a series of fittings so the suit will be just the right size, and then—"

"But I need this suit for a wedding tomorrow," the customer interrupts.

"Don't worry," says the salesman, "you'll have it!"

Smitty the bartender is suffering from a recurring ringing in his ears. It's driving him crazy, so finally he breaks down and goes to see a doctor.

The doctor gives him a thorough examination and tells him, "I am sorry to be the one to tell you this, but you have an incurable disease and you only have six months to live."

Since Smitty has no relatives, he decides to live it up in the little time he has left. He wants to spend every penny he has saved on having a good time. He plans a trip around the world. He wants a new wardrobe for his trip, so he goes to the best tailor and orders ten handmade suits, and he goes to a shirtmaker to have his shirts made to order.

The shirtmaker is measuring him. "Let's see, your sleeve measurement is thirty-four and your collar sixteen."

Smitty says, "No, I wear a fifteen collar."

The shirtmaker says, "Collar, sixteen. Look at the tape measure."

Smitty says, "It can't be; I've always worn a fifteen collar and that's what I want!"

And the shirtmaker says, "All right, but you'll get a ringing in your ears."

A lady is at the butcher counter in her neighborhood grocery store. She asks the butcher for a chicken, but before he cuts it up, she wants to look at it. She takes the chicken and examines the skin, she pinches the thighs to test its plumpness, then she takes the legs, pulls them apart, and sniffs at the bird.

"Sorry," she says to the butcher, "let me have another chicken."

The butcher gives her another chicken and she goes through the same routine; first she looks at the skin, then she pinches it, then she sniffs between its legs. Again she rejects the chicken and demands another one. The lady rejects all the chickens that the butcher offers her. Each time she goes through the same examination—looking at the skin, pinching it, and sniffing between the legs.

"Lady," the exasperated butcher says, "could *you* pass a test like that?"

A wealthy Texan is visiting a farm in Maine. The old farmer shows him around his property.

"Well," says the farmer, "my land extends just down the north forty there and over to the side to the stream over there and up around the top of that ridge."

"On my ranch," brags the Texan, "you can drive for two days and still not be at the end of my land."

The Maine farmer thinks for a moment and says, "Yeah, I had a car like that once!"

Three ministers are discussing how they divide the money they collect from their congregations. The first minister says, "What I do is draw a circle on the floor. I take the money and toss it in the air; anything than lands inside the circle goes to the church fund, and the money that lands outside the circle goes into my personal fund."

"I have a similar system," says the second minister. "I draw a line, then I throw the collection money into the air. The money that lands on the right side goes to the general church expenses, and the money that lands on the left side is used for my expenses."

"The way I do it," says the third minister, "is like this: I take all the money from the collection and I throw it into the air. Anything that God can catch, He keeps!"

Bernie the cabdriver is waiting for a fare at La Guardia Airport in New York. A man jumps into his cab and says, "I'll give you ten thousand dollars, including expenses, if you drive me to Paris, France."

Bernie thinks it over, then says, "I'm your man!" The cabbie drives to the docks, where a luxury liner is just getting ready to sail. He gets the captain to agree to let his cab on board and they cross the Atlantic to England. Once there, they cross over to France on a ferry. The cabbie drives nonstop until they get to Paris. He has been driving around the streets of Paris for no more than ten minutes when a guy jumps in his cab and says, "I'll give you $15,000 if you drive me to New York!"

Bernie can't believe his luck. He drives to the coast of France, takes a ferry to England, gets on an ocean liner, and sails back to New York. When he gets to Manhattan, the passenger says, "I'd like to go to this address in the Bronx."

"I'm sorry, Mac," says Bernie. "I don't go to the Bronx."

Charlie gets a call from his doctor and the doctor says, "I've got some good news and some bad news."

"Oh, no," says Charlie. "Doctor, tell me the good news first."

"You have an incurable disease and you'll be dead in twenty-four hours."

"My God," cries Charlie, "that's the good news! What's the bad news?"

"I was supposed to call you yesterday."

Jake is the owner of a manufacturing business. One day he discovers that one of his most trusted employees has stolen over a million dollars from the firm.

After much soul-searching, Jake goes to the man and says, "I don't want to create a scandal. I will just fire you and we will forget about the entire matter."

The employee says, "Fire me? Sure, it's true I've been stealing from you for years. How did you think I got that wonderful summer home, the cars, the jewelry? I have every luxury I ever dreamed of."

"So? Just give me one good reason I shouldn't fire you," demands Jake.

"Why hire someone new and have them start from scratch?"

Two men are sitting together on an airplane. The flight attendant comes up to them and asks, "Would you care for a cocktail?"

"Sure," says one man, "I'll take a martini."

"Certainly," says the flight attendant. "And what can I get for you?" she asks the other man.

"Young lady," he says, "before I touch strong drink, I'd just as soon commit adultery!"

"Oh, miss," says the first man, "as long as there's a choice, I'll have what he's having!"

A guy is late for a conference in New York because his plane is held up at Kennedy Airport. When he finally gets to his hotel, he learns that they have given the room he had reserved away because they were overbooked. He pleads with them and they say they can't possibly find him another room. Finally, the guys says, "Look, if the President of the United States came in here right now, would you find a room for him?"

"Well," says the room clerk, "I suppose if the President walked in, we could find him a room."

"Good," says the man. "The President can't make it. I'll take his room!"

In a small town in the Midwest, a salesman from New York is riding on a bus when he is shot to death.

The town sheriff is investigating the crime. He has several witnesses and the alleged perpetrator in his office. One man is telling him what happened. "This guy gets on the bus and sits down next to this pretty woman. He offers her twenty dollars to go with him to his hotel room. She is just red with embarrassment. He offers her thirty, then forty dollars.

"Then the woman jumps up and says, 'Isn't there a gentleman on this bus?'

"And that's when that man over there takes out a gun and shoots him."

The sheriff looks at the accused man and says, "Well, what's your story?"

"Well, Sheriff, I just couldn't sit still while some guy from out of town comes down here and tries to raise the prices!"

A bartender takes the advice of one of his customers, who happens to be an investment counselor. The counselor tells him, "Never take any action without consulting me first."

A few weeks later, the stock market crashes and the investment counselor walks into the bar. The bartender says, "You constantly tell me that you will advise me of the best action to take. So how should I act now?"

The counselor takes a sip of his beer and says, "Act broke."

A new hotel opens on the east side of Manhattan. The hotel prides itself on its exceptional service. Late one night, a guest calls room service.

"Hello, I would like a young virgin brought to my room," he says. "She should be eighteen and have long blond hair with pale blue eyes. I'll need some handcuffs and a nurse's uniform that's been dyed black. And also send up a bullfighter from Madrid, in full costume, of course, and make sure he's not over twenty-five. And if you could hurry, I'd appreciate it. I am tired and need to relax."

An hour goes by and the room-service captain calls back and says in an apologetic voice, "Sir, we have your handcuffs and the black nurse's uniform. It was a little bit tricky finding an eighteen-year-old virgin on such short notice, but we managed. But we are sorry to report that we were unable to find a bullfighter from Madrid. We do, however, have a twenty-two-year-old bullfighter from Mexico City. Will he do?"

"Certainly not," says the traveler. "So in that case, just send up some whole-wheat toast and some hot tea."

A Russian, a Cuban, an American businessman, and his lawyer are on the Orient Express traveling across Siberia. The Russian reaches into his suit-case and takes out a bottle of vodka. He pours each of his fellow travelers a glass, then throws the half-full bottle out the train window.

"Why did you do that?" asks the American businessman.

"Vodka flows like water in my country. We have more than we can ever drink," says the Russian.

Then the Cuban opens a box of premium Havana cigars. He offers one to each of the others. The Cuban takes a couple of puffs and tosses his lighted cigar out the window.

"Why did you throw a perfectly good cigar out the window?" asks the incredulous American.

"Cigars are so plentiful in my country," says the Cuban, "we have more of them then we know what to do with."

The American businessman is quiet for a moment, then he stands up, grabs the lawyer, and throws him out the window.

Henry rents a room in a boardinghouse and makes a deal with the landlady to pay a substan-tially higher rate if she will make lunch for him to take to work.

The first day she takes great pains to make a hearty lunch with a roast-beef sandwich loaded with meat as the main course. When Henry comes home from work, she asks how he liked the lunch. He replies, "Not bad . . . what there was of it."

The next day she makes two sandwiches. When he gets home, he has the same response to her ques-tion: "Not bad . . . what there was of it."

The next day the landlady takes a whole loaf of French bread, slices it down the middle, and loads it with three pounds of cold cuts. When Henry comes home from work that evening, he slams his lunch box down on the table and says, "Back to one sandwich again, I see!"

A new restaurant advertises that it will fill any order no matter how exotic or it will give you a thousand dollars. A man can't resist the offer and walks into the restaurant and asks the waiter for roasted ear of walrus on a buttered bun. The waiter disappears into the kitchen and returns with a check for one thousand dollars for the customer.

"I knew you wouldn't have walrus ears," he says triumphantly.

"Oh, we have walrus ears," says the waiter. "We just ran out of buns."

Donald walks into a bakery and tells the baker, "I would like a cake baked in the shape of the letter *B*."

"I can have it ready for you at about two this afternoon, but it will cost you."

"No problem," says Donald.

At two o'clock, Donald shows up at the bakery. The baker displays the cake to him in all its glory. Donald flies into a rage. "Not that kind of *B*, you idiot!" he screams. "I wanted a flowing *B* in script."

The baker retorts, "You didn't tell me that's what you wanted! I tell you what. I can give you that kind of cake, but it's gonna cost you. Come back at six."

Donald comes back at six and the baker shows him the cake. Donald studies it and says, "That's the shape I wanted, but I don't care for that frosting; could you frost it in a mocha flavor?"

"I can frost in mocha," says the baker. "Come

back at nine o'clock." At nine, Donald comes back and the cake is prepared to perfection. The baker is just about to put it in a box.

"Don't bother," says Donald, "I'll eat it here."

A guy who is a very hard worker gets his first job with the government. His office is quite impressive, with a view of the Potomac River. He begins behaving very strangely. After his first week on the job, he moves his desk into the space that is also occupied by his assistant's desk. Then a few days later, just before he leaves the office for the day, he shoves his desk out into the one of the many long corridors in the building. He works there for a few days and then he moves his desk into the men's room and sets up his office in there.

His odd behavior does not escape the notice of his fellow workers. It is strange to them, but they don't feel comfortable about saying anything to the man himself. Instead, they go to the department's psychiatrist.

The psychiatrist walks into the men's room and says, "The people you work with tell me you keep moving your desk. Tell me, why did you move it into the men's room?"

"Well," answers the man, "I figure that this is the only place in the government where they know what they are doing."

An unemployed New York actor goes to his agent and says, "I haven't had a job in three months; can't you find something for me?"

The agent looks through his files and says, "My God, here's a job I forgot to fill! It's only one line: 'Hark, I hear a cannon!' Can you be in Hartford, Connecticut, tonight?"

"I'm your man," says the actor.

He runs out of his agent's office and hails a cab. On the way to La Guardia Airport, he practices his line on the cabbie. "How does this sound?" he asks. " 'Hark . . . I hear a cannon.' "

"Not bad," says the cabdriver. "Just put a little more force into it when you say hark."

The actor jumps on the plane to Hartford. He's seated next to a businessman. The actor asks him what he thinks of his line, "Hark, I hear a cannon!"

"Use a little more body English when you deliver the line," suggests the businessman.

The actor runs off the plane; he makes it to the theater in ten minutes flat. All the time he is rehearsing his line, "Hark, I hear a cannon."

At the theater, the stage manager grabs him, rips off his clothes, puts him into a costume, and pushes him onto the stage. A huge blast of a cannon goes off just as the actor faces the audience.

He looks out across the footlights and says, "What the hell was that?"

A beautiful young woman is getting dressed for work one morning in her high-rise apartment building. She glances out her fiftieth-story bedroom window and sees a window washer outside. Thinking she will rattle him, she slowly takes off her dress. The window washer just goes about the business of cleaning the windows. Next, she removes her slip in a very provocative manner. Still, the man just keeps working away. Taking her striptease to the full extent, she takes off her bra and panties and begins parading around her room. The window washer still takes no notice of her. Finally, the woman walks over to the window and just stands there, totally naked, staring at the man outside her window.

At last the window washer puts down his pail and says, "What's the matter, lady, haven't you ever seen a window washer before?"

A tourist is visiting Africa when he comes upon an old witch doctor who is lying in the road with his ear to the ground. The tourist walks a little closer and overhears the witch doctor saying, "White man! In Jeep! Women in car, too. He wear plaid shirt."

"That's incredible!" says the tourist. "Can you tell all that just by putting your ear to the ground?"

"No," cries the witch doctor. "Run over me!"

Each Saturday, old Mrs. O'Malley goes to Confession at St. Patrick's Church. Mrs. O'Malley is very deaf, and when she is confessing her sins, she has a tendency to shout. The priest suggests that she speak more quietly, since everyone in the church can hear what she was saying. Finally, the priest tells Mrs. O'Malley that it might be a good idea to write her sins down in advance.

The next Saturday Mrs. O'Malley kneels down in the confessional and hands the priest a piece of paper. The priest puts on his reading glasses, looks at the paper, and says, "What's this? It looks like a grocery list."

"Oh, my God!" says Mrs. O'Malley. "I must have left my sins at the 7-Eleven."

Bill is selling tickets at the local train station when a young man approaches him. "I'd like a round-trip ticket," says the man.

"Where to?" asks Bill.

The man looks confused and says, "Well, to here, of course."

Bob gets off a commuter train in a suburban town. He walks over to the nearby office of the local town doctor. The stranger tells the doctor that his wife is very ill; it is an emergency. Bob pleads with the doctor to make a house call. The doctor agrees to see the woman and Bob and the doctor gets into the doctor's car and drive to the outskirts of town. As they pull into the man's driveway Bob asks the doctor if he could pay him in advance.

The doctor thinks this is a peculiar request, but he agrees, saying, "My fee is forty dollars."

Bob takes out his wallet and pays the doctor. Then, red-faced, he says to the doctor, "My wife is feeling fine; you really don't need to come inside."

The bewildered doctor demands an explanation. "It's like this, doctor," admits the guy. "Those crooks at the cabstand near the train wanted fifty-five dollars to drive me out here, and I heard you were cheaper!"

An actor, who has been unemployed for months, is desperate for work. He's looking through the want ads and he comes across a position with the local zoo.

"Here's the deal," explains the zoo manager when the actor arrives at his office. "We've advertised that we have two gorillas at our zoo, but one of the apes just died. We hate to disappoint all the young kids who will be coming here expecting to see two gorillas. All you have to do is put on this gorilla suit and sit in the cage."

The man puts on the furry costume and is sitting

in the cage eating a banana when the door opens and another gorilla is shoved in with him.

"Get me outta here!" yells the actor, shaking the bars of the cage.

"Keep quiet," says the other gorilla. "You think you're the only actor out of work?"

A guy is weary of his hectic life. He decides to join a group of Buddhist monks in a remote monastery high in the mountains in India. The monks are very strict. They sit and contemplate their navels. Each monk takes a vow of silence. Once every ten years, they meet with the head monk and are allowed to speak three words.

Ten years pass and the guy is called into the head monk's chambers. "My son," the monk says, "do you have anything to say?"

The man nods his head and says, "Food's no good."

The old monk nods and notes it in an ancient leather-bound book.

Another ten years pass and the elder monk summons the guy into his chambers once more. "You have been with us now for twenty years, is there anything you would like to say on this occasion?"

"Bed's too hard," says the guy as he bows to the elder monk.

The monk nods and again takes out the tattered book and writes in it.

Finally, thirty years have passed and the guy is once more called into the monk's chambers. "Another decade has passed, what do you have to say?" asks the elder monk.

"I want out!" says the guy.

"Well, it's about time," says the monk. "You've done nothing but complain since you got here."

A customer is complaining to his barber about the price of haircuts. "I just got back from London, and over there I got a good haircut for five dollars."

The barber says, "Yeah, but look at the airfare."

Tony walks into a psychiatrist's office and says, "Doc, I'm going crazy. I keep imagining I am a zebra. Every time I look at myself in the mirror, I see my entire body covered with black-and-white stripes."

The doctor says, "Now calm down; go home and take these pills, get a good night's sleep, and I am sure the black stripes will disappear."

Tony takes the pills and comes back the next day. He says, "Doc, I feel great. Got anything for the white stripes."

A carpenter wakes up with a sore thumb. He goes to see his doctor. After an examination, the doctor says, "Go home and soak it in cold water."

He goes home and is soaking his thumb in a pan of cold water when his wife walks in. She says, "What are you doing?"

"My thumb's been hurting and the doctor told me to soak it in cold water."

"What?" says his wife. "I'm telling you to soak it in hot water."

The guy takes his wife's advice and soaks his thumb in hot water, and the next day it's all healed.

The following week, he runs into his doctor. He says, "You know, doctor, you told me to soak my thumb in cold water and my wife told me hot water. I took her advice and soaked it in the hot water and it got better."

"I'm sorry," says the doctor. "*My* wife says cold water!"

A criminal with a long record of convictions is being sentenced once more. The judge says, "You've been found guilty on two counts. I am sentencing you to two life sentences to be served consecutively." The prisoner bursts into tears. The judge softens and says, "Okay, so I may be a bit harsh. I hereby cut your sentence in half."

An old man named Bill is explaining to his young assistant how he made a fortune as a paint contractor even though he can't read or write. "I owe it all to the father of my first girlfriend," says the old man.

"Did he give you your first painting job?"

"In a way he did. My girlfriend told me her father went to bed at eleven, so I decided to sneak into her bedroom at eleven-thirty. I put the ladder against the side of her house. When I got halfway to her bedroom, her father stuck his head out the window and saw me!"

"What did you do then?"

"What else could I do? I started painting the house."

An out-of-work bartender is desperate for money and he goes door-to-door asking people if they need any painting done. He rings the doorbell of a house and a man comes to the door.

"Excuse me, sir, but I was wondering if you needed anything painted?"

The man says, "What incredible timing. I was just about to paint my porch out back."

"I'm your man," answers the guy.

"I've already washed the porch, so you can get started right away."

Three hours pass and the guy finishes the job. He is collecting his money and he says to the man, "I did a great job! Every inch is painted snow white. And by the way, it's a Ferrari not a Porsche."

John and his wife go to a wine auction where he buys a bottle of turn-of-the-century French wine for fifteen thousand dollars. It's late at night when John and his wife drive home. As they get out of the car he's holding the expensive bottle of wine. Just as he's stepping over the curb he trips and falls and there's a terrible crunching noise.

"What's broken?" asks his wife.

"I don't know, but I'm feeling something wet."

"Oh, no," cries his wife. "Let's hope it's blood."

An insurance adjuster is interviewing a man who has filed a claim after his house burned to the ground.

"Were you smoking in bed?" the adjuster asks.

"Of course not," says the man. "The bed was on fire when I climbed into it."

A small spaceship crash-lands in New York City just opposite the famous Stage Door Delicatessen. A Martian manages to struggle out of the ship and is inspecting the damage. While he's doing this he sees the bagels in the deli's window. He goes inside and says to the clerk, "Can I have one of those wheels for my spaceship?"

The clerk says, "Those aren't wheels. They're bagels; you eat them. Here, try one." And he hands a bagel to the Martian.

The Martian eats the bagel and says, "You know, these would be great with cream cheese!"

Two state troopers are cruising down the highway when they spot a driver who is driving in perfect adherence to the law: the car is clocked at exactly 55 mph, signals when changing lanes, and keeps the ideal distance from the cars in front. The cops decide they would feel good if this once they stopped a driver and commended him for obeying the law. They follow the car home and a little old lady gets out of the car and is walking into her house.

"Excuse me," says one of the cops. "We want to congratulate you on your driving. You are a good cautious driver."

"Oh, thank you, officers," says the little old lady. "I have to be extra careful ever since they took my license away for failing the eye exam."

A minister is awakened one night by a knock at the door. Standing there is a man who is cold and hungry. An inner voice speaks to the minister and says, "Let him in and feed him."

The minister takes the man into the kitchen and makes him something to eat. Sitting at the table, they get into a lively conversation about theology. The stranger says, "I don't believe in God and I never will!" The two of them get into a heated debate about the existence of God, and finally, the minister can stand it no longer and throws the man out into the night.

Just as the minister is about to fall asleep an inner voice says to him, "Why did you send that man away?"

"But God," says the minister, "didn't You hear all the terrible things he was saying about You?"

"Listen," says God, "I've put up with the SOB for fifty years. You could have stood him for one night."

Down on the farm, it is young Matt's chore to milk the family cow and carry a fresh pail of milk to his aunt Mary. One day Matt plays a trick on his aunt and spikes the milk with a shot of whiskey. His aunt enjoys the flavor so much that he continues spiking the milk. One morning he oversleeps, and when he finally gets up, he finds his aunt Mary waiting for him at her door. She grabs a cupful of the milk and says to Matt, "Tell your father whatever he does, don't sell that cow!"

A guy is giving a speech at his lodge meeting. He gets a bit carried away and talks for two hours. Finally, he realizes what he is doing and says, "I'm sorry I talked so long, I left my watch at home."

A voice from the back of the room says, "There's a calendar behind you!"

A moonshiner is on trial in Georgia for illegally running a still in the mountains. The judge turns to the jury and says, "Are there any questions members of the jury would like to ask before considering the evidence?"

"A few of us, Your Honor," says the foreman, "would like to know if the defendant boiled the mash for two or three hours, and how he keeps the yeast out."

Larry knocks on the door of an elderly lady. The old lady opens the door and Larry says, "Excuse me, madam, I represent the town council and we are taking up a collection for the betterment of the—"

"You'll have to speak up," interrupts the old lady. "I am hard of hearing."

Larry talks a little louder. "I represent the town council and we are taking up a collection for the better—"

"I can't hear you," says the old lady.

He tries again. *"I represent the town council and we are taking up a collection—"*

"What's that you say?" says the old lady.

"I REPRESENT THE TOWN COUNCIL AND WE ARE TAKING UP A COLLECTION—"

"Can't hear a thing," says the old lady.

Irritated, Larry storms down the walkway and slams the garden gate. "Young man," says the old lady, "please don't do that to my gate."

"Screw the gate," he says under his breath.

"Oh, yeah," says the old lady, "screw the town council."

A man who owns an optical shop is telling his son how to charge customers. "I use the flinch method," says the optometrist. "Let me show you with this customer.

"There you are, sir, I've finished fitting you with the glasses," he says.

The man says, "How much will it be?"

"That will be fifty dollars," says the eye doctor. He waits a few seconds and the customer doesn't flinch.

"For the frames; the lens will be another fifty," says the optometrist. Again the doctor waits and still the customer doesn't flinch.

Then eye doctor says, "Each."

A lawyer is working late at night on a difficult case when in a puff of smoke the devil appears to him. The devil offers to make him the most powerful, wealthiest lawyer in the history of the world.

"I'll bet," says the lawyer, "and all I have to do is give you my soul."

"No," says the devil, "I only ask the right to damn to eternal suffering the souls of your wife and two young children!"

The man is dumbstruck, thinks for a moment, then looks at the devil. "All right," he says, "but what's the catch?"

Barreling down the highway is a truck with a double-deck load of new cars. Just about dusk, the truck driver realizes his headlights aren't working. At the next truck stop, he gets out of the truck, climbs onto the top deck, and turns on the headlights of the car in front. Then he drives back onto the darkened highway. He is heading down the road when a driver coming in the opposite direction slams on his brakes and deliberately drives his car off the road into a ditch. The truck driver stops and walks over to the ditch. The driver is standing near his car, dazed.

"What the hell did you drive off the road for?" asks the truck driver.

"When I saw your headlights, I figured if your truck is as wide as it is high I'd better give you the whole road."

An exclusive New York hotel prides itself on having the most luxurious rooms in the city. Late one night, a man comes down to the lobby to complain.

"I just don't understand, sir," says the desk

clerk. "We've been in business now for three years and you are the first guest to complain. Our rooms are furnished with the most expensive antiques, each bath has gold fixtures and is made of Italian marble. We provide you with a complete bar, including imported French wine. I just don't understand what could be wrong. Please tell me, what is the problem?"

"Well, for one thing," says the man, "the room's on fire."

A psychiatrist has group therapy each Wednesday night and he thinks he will try an experiment with the small group. He pours water from a pitcher into a metal bucket and then asks each member of the group what the sound reminds them of.

The first man says, "It makes me think of being a child on the farm; it sounds like the noise the rain made on the roof when we had a thunderstorm."

"Good," says the psychiatrist.

"To me," says the second man, "it sounds like a beautiful waterfall that I saw when I went on vacation in Hawaii."

"Good," says the psychiatrist.

"Makes me think of sex," says the third man.

"Why, did you have your first sexual experience in the rain?" asks the psychiatrist.

"No," says the man. "Everything makes me think of sex."

A carpenter has a mad compulsion that he can't seem to control. Each day he steals lumber from the job site. The more he tries to control himself, the more difficult the problem becomes. Finally, the man goes to Confession. "Father, forgive me, but I steal lumber. I don't mean to do it, I just can't help myself."

"I understand," says the priest. "For your penance, please make a act of contrition."

"Father," says the man, "I've never made one before. But if you have the plans, I have the lumber."

A witness is called in to testify about a traffic accident. The lawyer asks the witness, "Did you actually see the car accident?"

"Yes, I did."

"And how far away were you when you saw the two cars collide?"

The guy says, "I was twenty-nine feet and six and three quarter inches away."

The lawyer pauses for a moment, thinking he's got the better of the witness. "How can you be sure you were exactly twenty-nine feet and six and three quarters inches away?"

"Because," says the man, "when it happened, I took out a tape measure and checked the distance . . . because I knew that some damn lawyer was going to ask me that question."

A large truck loaded with structural steel beams drives under a low bridge and gets stuck halfway through. The truck driver tries everything he can think of to free himself. Nothing works. As a last resort, he even lets the air out of his tires, and still the truck wouldn't budge.

Finally, a police car drives by and the cop says, "Are you stuck?"

"No," says the driver, "I'm delivering this bridge and I lost the address."

Bill goes into a clothing store and says to the owner, "I need a job really bad, can you hire me as a salesman?"

The owner says, "I'm going out to lunch. If you can sell that ugly plaid suit while I'm gone, I'll give you the job."

The suit is the worst-looking thing Bill has ever seen, but he's desperate, so he agrees to do it. An hour later, the owner returns and the store is in a shambles: racks are turned over, the clothes are all over the floor—but the plaid suit is sold.

The owner says, "What happened? Did you have some kind of trouble here?"

"I had no trouble with the guy who bought the suit, but what a tough Seeing Eye dog."

George the bartender and his wife are always fighting about money. Finally, George decides to let his wife handle the money. Two months later, she tells him that she got rid of something that they never use. She has saved so much money that they can go on vacation.

They spend the next two weeks in Maui at a first-class hotel. They eat dinner each night in the best restaurants on the island. They rent a sailboat and cruise to the outer islands. They are having the time of their lives. Then George has an accident on the sailboat and breaks his leg. He's in the hospital when his wife comes to visit and she's very upset.

"Don't worry," says George, "I'll be out of here in no time."

She says, "I sure hope so. Remember when I told you I got rid of something I never use? It was our hospital insurance."

A guy is visiting here from another country and speaks very little English. He gets on a bus downtown and says to the driver, "Park Avenue! Park Avenue!"

The driver nods to the guy and points to the fare box. The guy leans over and shouts into the fare box, *"Park Avenue, Park Avenue."*

Jill lands in New York after spending a few weeks in Paris. She is going through customs when the agent asks her, "Cognac? Cigarettes? French wine? Liqueurs? Designer clothing?"

"No thanks," says Jill. "A cup of coffee would be just fine."

Jerry is having a few friends over to watch the big game on TV. The Forty-Niners score a touchdown and the guy gets up and leans out the window and yells, "Green side up, green side up."

In the next quarter, the Niners score a field goal and Jerry goes to the window and yells, "Green side up, green side up."

They are all engrossed in the game and a commercial comes on. Jerry runs to the window and yells, "Green side up, green side up."

"What are you doing?" asks one of his friends. "Relax and watch the game. Why do you keep yelling out the window 'green side up'?"

"I can't relax," says Jerry. "I hired a bunch of college kids to put in my lawn."

Bill and his friend Stan are out on the golf course when they run into Arnold Palmer. Stan says, "I know Arnold Palmer." As soon as Arnie spots Stan, he walks over and shakes his hand and they talk about old times.

"I can't believe you know Arnold Palmer," says Bill.

"Oh, that's nothing," says Stan. "I am a very close personal friend of George and Barbara Bush."

"No way," says Bill.

"I'll show you," says Stan. He picks up the telephone in the clubhouse and calls the Bushes. The next thing you know, *Air Force One* has landed at a nearby airport and Stan and his friend are in Kennebunkport fishing with the President. The President even asks Stan his advice about the economy. Bill can't believe that Stan knows the President.

"That's nothing," says Stan when they return home. "I am very close to the Pope."

"This can't be true," Bill says.

"I'll show you."

The two men fly to Italy and they are standing in the square in front of the Vatican. The Pope is about to come out and give his blessing to the crowd when Stan disappears. A few minutes later, the Pope is standing on the balcony and Stan is right there beside him with his arm around the Pope's shoulder.

Bill can't believe his eyes, and before he can say anything, the man standing next to him says, "Excuse me, do you know who that guy is who's standing next to Stan?"

A man becomes interested in his family tree and looks up the phone number of a genealogist in the Yellow Pages. "Tell me," he asks, "how much will it cost me to research my family tree."

"It will be in the neighborhood of two to three thousand dollars."

"That much?" says the man. "Isn't there a way to do it for free?"

"Sure, run for president."

A foreman of a match company is just about to leave work for the day when he gets a call from the President of the United States.

"You are being presented with the Congressional Medal of Honor," says the President.

The guy can't believe it, but the next day he's standing in the Rose Garden with the President and being given the highest medal in the land.

"Last week," says the President, "terrorists tried to burn down a weapons depository in the West and they didn't succeed."

"But, Mr. President," asks the foreman, "why are you giving me this medal?"

"The matches failed to light."

Liz goes to her first show at an art gallery and is looking at the paintings. One is a huge canvas that has black with yellow blobs of paint splattered all over it. The next painting is a murky gray color that has drips of purple paint streaked across it. Liz walks over to the artist and says, "I don't understand your paintings."

"I paint what I feel inside me," explains the artist.

"Have you ever tried Alka-Seltzer?"

Shirley and Sally are grocery shopping. Shirley picks up a jar of olives and puts them in her cart.

"I didn't know you liked olives," says Sally.

"I never did," says Shirley, "until I tried them with this great recipe with gin and vermouth."

The cops make a sweep of downtown and bring twenty-five hookers into court. The judge asks the first woman what she does for a living. "I'm a schoolteacher, Your Honor."

The judge asks each woman in turn how she earns a living. Each time he gets the same answer: "I'm a schoolteacher."

Finally, he asks the twenty-fifth woman what she does and the woman looks him squarely in the eye and says, "I'm a hooker."

Impressed with her honesty, the judge says, "How's business?"

"Well, Your Honor," she answers, "it would be a hell of a lot better if there weren't so many schoolteachers around."

Barbara reads in *Vogue* that bathing in milk is good for the skin. She decides to give it a try and calls the local dairy. "I would like fifty gallons of milk delivered to my house. I am going to bathe in it."

The man at the dairy says, "Would you like it pasteurized?"

"No, just up to my chin."

A preacher is giving one of his hellfire-and-damnation sermons. He says in a loud voice, "If anyone has partaken of sin this week, let him stand up and present himself."

A little old lady in the back row looks around and then shrugs her shoulders and stands up.

"I can't believe my eyes," says the preacher. "You, Sister Rose, are guilty of sin?"

"Oh, sin!" says Rose. "I thought you said *gin*."

While George is in France he comes up with a scam for smuggling French wine into the United States without paying any duty. He dresses like a priest. He has hundreds of bottles of wine labeled with a picture of a cross. As he's going through customs the agent says to him, "What's in the bottles?"

"Why, that's holy water from Lourdes in France."

The agent opens one of the bottles, smells the contents, and says, "This isn't water, it's wine."

"Praise the Lord, it's another miracle."

It's a hot muggy day in Egypt. A galleyful of slaves are rowing Cleopatra's barge down the Nile. The captain comes down to the hold and announces to all the slaves, "I have some good news and some bad news. First, the good news! You will have the morning off. You can relax and do whatever you want. Also, you will be feasting at the royal dining table for lunch. Eat as much as you want."

"What's the bad news?" yells out one of the slaves.

"This afternoon, Cleopatra wants to go water-skiing."

A guy is on a tour of a nudist colony. One guy with a beard down to his knees is sitting in the corner.

"Who's that?" asks the visitor.

"That's Fuzzy! Someone has to go out for coffee."

A lawyer, a Jew, and a Hindu are traveling together and they are caught in a terrible snowstorm. They make their way to a farmhouse. The farmer says, "I'll let you stay here, but one of you will have to sleep in the barn."

First the Hindu goes out to the barn, and in a few minutes, there is a knock on the farmhouse door. The Hindu says, "In my country, cows are a sacred animal. It would be a terrible sin for me to sleep in the same place as a cow."

Then the Jew heads for the barn. In no time, there is a knock at the farmhouse door. The Jew says, "I'd stay in the barn, but my religion forbids me from sleeping with a pig."

The lawyer had no choice and he heads for the barn. A few minutes later, there is a knock on the farmhouse door and there stand the pig and the cow.

Rick has had a terrible cold for weeks. Finally, he goes to see his doctor. The doctor prescribes some medicine, but it doesn't work. Rick comes back and the doctor recommends that he take the week off work. Rick complies, but at the end of the week, he still has the cold. He goes back one more time and the doctor tells him, "Go home and fill your bathtub full of icy cold water, soak in it for an hour. Then go outside and stand in your yard totally naked and let the wind blow you dry."

"But, doc," says Rick, "I'll catch pneumonia!"

"I know! I can cure pneumonia."

An accounting company buys a gigantic computer. It takes up a whole wall in the small company. Two of the company's accountants are giving it a trial run. They feed the complex accounting problem into the computer, and in a few minutes a small piece of paper spits out the answer. They study the paper gravely and one guy turns to the other and says, "Do you realize that it would take 400 ordinary accountants 350 years to make a mistake this big."

A Canadian lumber camp advertises for a lumberjack. A skinny little guy shows up at the camp the next day carrying an ax. The head lumberjack takes one look at the puny little guy and tells him to get lost.

"Give me a chance to show you what I can do," says the skinny guy.

"See that giant redwood over there?" says the lumberjack. "Take your ax and cut it down."

The guy heads for the tree, and in five minutes he's knocking on the lumberjack's door. "I cut the tree down," says the guy.

The lumberjack can't believe his eyes and says, "Where did you learn to chop down trees like that?"

"In the Sahara Forest," says the puny man.

"You mean the Sahara Desert," says the lumberjack.

"Sure, that's what they call it now."

A tribe of cannibals finds a stack of magazines left behind by some tourists. The old chief is looking through a catalog of women's sexy underwear. Every few pages he tears out a page and stuffs it in his mouth and eats it.

Finally, his son asks him, "What do you think, Dad? Is that dehydrated stuff any good?"

Old man Finnigan and his wife are sitting in Smitty's Bar watching the baseball game on television. Finnigan's wife turns to her husband and says, "Honey, I could really go for a corned-beef sandwich."

"I'll run out after this inning and get it for you," says Finnigan.

"You know how you are. Why don't you write it down so you don't forget."

"I won't forget," he protests.

"I want a corned beef on rye bread. Please write it down."

"Don't worry, I won't forget."

"And just a little mustand. Don't have him put on too much."

"Got it, not too much mustard."

"And don't forget the pickle; are you sure you don't want to write it down, there's a lot to remember?"

"Elephants could take memory lessons from me," says Finnigan as he walks out the door to buy the sandwich.

He comes back a little while later and hands his wife an ice-cream cone.

His distraught wife bursts into tears. "I told you to write it down. I wanted chocolate not vanilla."

6

LAST CALL

When you are having fun with good friends, the time just slips away. We just checked our watch, and sorry to say, folks, it's time to close. So this is our last call. . . . One more laugh for the road.

Mr. and Mrs. Weatherby are up before the judge. "And how can I help you folks?" asks the judge.

"We want a divorce," says old man Weatherby.

"If I may ask, how old are you?"

"Well, judge, I am ninety-five and my wife is ninety-three," he answers.

"And how long have you been married?" continues the judge.

"Seventy years last April, Your Honor," says the old lady.

"Why do you want to get a divorce now?"

"We wanted to wait until the children were dead!"

Dressed in black, Bob is walking with a large pit bull on a leash. Bob and the dog are following a hearse. Bob has his head bowed as he leads a large group of mourners down the street. A curious neighbor watching this sad sight walks across the street, approaches Bob, and says, "Excuse me, I know this isn't the time to talk, but could you tell me what happened?"

"It's my lawyer and his partner; they both died."

"How awful. If it isn't too painful to talk about, how did it happen?"

"My dog; he killed them."

"Oh, I am sorry to hear that," says the neighbor. After a few minutes of thinking it over, he asks, "Say, mind if I borrow your dog?"

"Sure, get in line."

A bartender dies and has his body frozen. He comes back to life fifty years later. The first thing he does is find a pay phone and calls his broker to see how his investments are doing. The broker says, "Your IBM is worth six thousand dollars a share. The AT&T is now valued at seven thousand a share, and your GM is going for ten thousand a share."

The bartender says, "I'm a millionaire, this is great." Just then the operator breaks in and says, "Your first three minutes are up . . . please deposit another five hundred dollars."

A governor of an eastern state is sound asleep late one night when he is awakened by a phone call from a very ambitious civil servant. "Mr. Governor, I am sorry to wake you up at this time, but your state auditor has just died and I would like to know if I could take his place."

The governor, fully awake now, thinks it over and answers, "I guess it's all right with me, if it's all right with the undertaker."

Gil, a very devout man who has total faith in God, lives in a house by a river. One day there is a terrible flood and Gil climbs on top of his roof to be saved from drowning.

An hour goes by and a boat comes by to rescue him. Gil refuses, saying to the man in the boat, "I have faith that God will rescue me!" The wind is whipping around and the water is rising and another boat comes by to save him. Again he refuses to get in the boat, saying, "I have faith in my Maker, he will save me." Another hour goes by and a helicopter flies over the house and they lower a rope to him. Gil waves the helicopter away, shouting, "I have faith in God to rescue me."

At last, the force of the water is so great that it tears the house apart and Gil drowns. He goes up to heaven. When he reaches the Pearly Gates, he asks St. Peter, "Why did I drown? I had such faith in God, how could He let me down?"

"What do you mean, He let you down? He sent you two boats and a helicopter."

Phil is not feeling very well and goes to the doctor. After giving him a thorough checkup, the doctor shakes his head and says, "It seems you need a brain transplant."

"You're the doctor," says Phil, "but aren't they kind of expensive."

"The price varies quite a bit," answers the doctor. "It really depends on what type of brain you get."

"What are my choices?"

"I can give you the brain of a lawyer; they run about $30,000 on the current market. Or you may want the brain of a doctor; they are selling for about $60,000. Or if you want the brain of a politician, that will run about $120,000."

"How come the brain of a politician costs twice as much as a doctor's brain?" demands Phil.

"That's because the politician's brain has never been used."

A large firm offers its employees an opportunity to join a pension plan with excellent benefits, but there is one condition. Every employee has to sign up for the plan and they all have to sign within one month. Lines form in every department to sign up for the plan. Within a few days, everyone in the company is signed up except for one employee, Jim Smith.

Everyone in the company argues with him—his secretary, his coworkers, and his supervisor. But Jim won't budge.

"I just don't get it, it's too complicated to understand," he tells those who argue with him.

The deadline is approaching, and finally, Jim is sent to see the president of the firm. A copy of the pension plan and a pen are sitting on his desk.

"Mr. Smith," the president begins, "I have discussed this with your supervisor. As you can see, we are on the tenth floor of the building. If you do not sign this paper, I personally will throw you out the window."

Without hesitating, Jim picks up the pen and signs the paper. The president glares at him and says, "Tell me, why didn't you sign the pension plan before?"

"Well, to be honest with you, you're the first one who explained it to me."

An old man is very sick; he's nearing the end. He calls his son to his bedside. "Son," the dying man says, "I know we have had our differences over the years, but I want you to rest assured that when I go, you will get everything—the stocks, the big house on the hill, the summer home by the ocean, my cars, all my money, everything! It's all yours."

His son says, "Dad, I never expected this moment to come. I am so grateful to you. Is there anything I can do? Anything at all?"

"Yes," says the old man, "I'd appreciate it if you would take your foot off the oxygen hose."

Two prisoners are up against the wall, their hands tied behind their backs, waiting to be shot.

The officer in charge comes forward; he says to them, "Do you want a final cigarette?"

One prisoner spits at the officer and says, "Keep your filthy cigarette, you disgusting dog."

The second prisoner whispers, "Bill, don't make trouble."

A dyslexic cop is severely reprimanded by his captain because the spelling on his police reports is incomprehensible. "How can you expect anyone to read this! If you file just one more report with any—and I mean any—words misspelled, you are going on report!" screams the captain.

The cop vows not to make any more mistakes. The next day he is in his patrol car when a report of a traffic accident comes over his two-way radio. He arrives on the scene to discover a grisly head-on collision. The cop takes out his notebook and begins to write, taking care to spell each word correctly.

"One, O-N-E. Ford, F-O-R-D. In the ditch, D-I-T-C-H."

"That's good," thinks the cop as he walks across the street to the other vehicle.

"One, O-N-E. Dodge, D-O-D-G-E. In the ditch, D-I-T-C-H.

"I am doing great!" says the cop out loud as he confidently walks to the middle of the highway, where he discovers a decapitated head.

"One, O-N-E. Head, H-E-A-D. In the boulevard, B-U-L . . . B-L-U . . . B-O-L-L . . . B-I-L . . ."

Finally, the frustrated cop looks around, then kicks the head with his boot, and writes, "One head in the D-I-T-C-H."

The bell ringer in the local church dies, so the pastor puts an ad in the newspaper for a replacement. The next day he hears a terrible noise at the door. The pastor opens the door and there stands a man who has no arms.

The armless man says, "I've come about the job."

The pastor says, "My good man, how could you possibly ring the bell?"

"I'll show you," answers the man. Before the pastor can stop him, the man hurries to the bell tower. He positions himself in front of the bell and counts to ten, then he aims his head at the bell and runs into it with all his force. There is a great *Gong!* The bell swings back and forth and hits the bell ringer and he falls out of the tower onto the concrete sidewalk below. The pastor rushes to his side to say some prayers.

A concerned bystander says to the pastor, "Who is that man?"

The pastor replies, "I don't know his name, but his face rings a bell."

A few days later, the pastor again hears a terrible noise at his door. He opens it and discovers another man with no arms, who claims to be the twin of the deceased bell ringer. He asks for the job. The armless man begs the pastor to let him try out for the position. Then he scurries up to the bell tower, puts his head down, and runs at the bell. This time the bell ringer misses the bell and falls out of the tower and lands on the sidewalk. The pastor rushes down to offer some prayers.

A bystander says to the pastor, "Who is that man?"

The pastor replies, "I don't know, but he's a dead ringer for that other guy."

At a meeting in Cuba where Fidel Castro is presiding, one of the men present, José Valdez, gets up and says, "I have three questions. If things are so great in Cuba, what happened to all the jobs? If Cuba is such a great agricultural country, what happened to all the food? And if Cuba is the land of freedom, what happened to our right to leave?"

Castro can hardly believe what he has heard. He answers, "It is too late to answer your questions. At our next meeting, I will respond to all your questions."

At the next meeting, one of the members stands up and says, "I have just one question. . . . What happened to José Valdez?"

A lawyer dies and goes to meet his Maker. When he gets to the Pearly Gates, St. Peter, Moses, and God are all lined up waiting to meet him. There is an orchestra of ten thousand angels playing on their harps. A large white cake with his name on it is waiting to be cut. St. Peter rushes over to shake his hand.

"Does everyone get a welcome like this?" asks the lawyer.

"No, you are very special," St. Peter says. "We've never had anyone who lived to be 130 before."

The lawyer is puzzled. "But I'm only 45."

St. Peter thinks for a moment, then says, "Wouldn't you know! We must have added up your billing hours."

A wealthy store owner is on his deathbed and has asked his three favorite customers—a butcher, a cop, and a bartender—to discuss his estate.

"I have no family," he begins, "so I am dividing my wealth among the three of you, in three equal parts. As a sign of our friendship and trust, I would like each of you to make a token gesture, after I'm gone, by putting a thousand dollars in my coffin before I am lowered into the ground."

Several days later, the funeral is conducted, according to the wishes of the deceased. At the appointed time, the butcher walks up and puts an envelope containing the thousand in the coffin. Next, the cop puts his envelope in the coffin. Then the bartender walks up to the coffin. He takes out the two envelopes and replaces them with a check for three thousand.

Two guys are riding down the highway when suddenly the driver pulls over to the side of the road. He says, "Ya know, I'm not so sure my directional signals are working. Stand behind the car and let me know."

The other guy gets out of the car and stands there without saying anything. Finally, the driver shouts, "What's happening?"

"They're working . . . they're not working . . . they're working . . . they're not working. . . ."

Sam invents a new computer. He claims it will answer any question. A prospective buyer sits down in front of it and types in his question: "Where is my father?"

The computer prints out on the laser printer: "Your father is fishing in Montana."

The guy turns to the inventor and says, "This thing is useless; my father's been dead for ten years."

Sam says, "I don't understand what's gone wrong. Try rephrasing your question."

The guy types: "Where is the man my mother married? Come on, tell me what my father is doing."

The printer prints: "Your mother's husband is dead. Your father just landed a three-pound trout."

Bill is arguing with the devil. Satan claims no one on earth has a perfect memory. But Bill says there is an Indian he knows who never forgets anything. Bill agrees to give his soul to the devil if the Indian ever forgets anything.

The devil goes up to the Indian and says, "Do you like eggs?"

"Yes," says the Indian.

Twenty years later, Bill dies. The devil thinks, "Now's my chance to claim his soul." He goes down to earth and finds the old Indian. The devil raises his hand and says, "How."

The Indian says, "Scrambled."

A guy who doesn't speak English robs a bank with a bunch of other guys. He runs away from the other men and takes all the money and hides it. The other robbers hunt him down and capture him.

They have an interpreter tell him, "If you don't tell us where the money is, we are going to cut off both your feet."

The guy tells the interpreter, "Tell them I forgot where I hid the money." They take him out and cut off his feet.

Then they ask the interpreter to say to him, "If you don't tell us where the money is, we are going to cut off both your hands."

The man says to the interpreter, "Tell them I don't remember where the money is."

They take him and cut off both his hands. Then they tell the interpreter to tell him, "If you don't tell us where the money is, we are going to cut off your head."

The man finally breaks down and tells the interpreter, "The money is buried under an oak tree behind an old shack just north of my house."

The interpreter says to the group of bandits, "He says he'd rather die than tell you where the money is!"

An out-of-work ventriloquist decides to set up shop as a psychic. The business gets off to a shaky start, but one day a woman comes to him dressed in black. She asks him, "Can you put me in touch with my dead husband, Ralph."

"No problem."

And for the next hour, the lady has a lively conversation with her dead husband, Ralph. The woman is so happy that instead of the fifty-dollar fee she insists on paying the man five hundred dollars.

The ventriloquist is so excited he says, "This is

great! And just to show you how much I appreciate it, the next time you talk with your dead husband, Ralph, I'm going to drink a glass of water at the same time."

Al dies and goes to hell. The devil asks him, "Which part of hell would you like to be admitted to?"

Al says, "There's a choice?"

"Of course," says the devil. He takes Al down a long corridor and asks him to listen at each door before he makes his decision.

At the first door, Al hears terrible moans of pain. He goes to the second door and hears screams of despair. At each door all he hears are cries and screams. Finally, he comes to a door, puts his ear to it, and hears gentle murmuring.

Quick as a wink he says, "I'll take that door."

The door is flung open and he's thrown inside. Suddenly he's up to his lips in a vast sea of human waste. With him are millions of others standing on their tiptoes, murmuring, "Don't make waves! Don't make waves!"

Three men—an American, an Englishman, and a German—are sentenced to death by the French government. Guards lead the American to the guillotine. "Do you have any last words?"

He says, "God bless America." They put his head on the block and let the blade fall. Halfway down, the blade gets stuck.

They tell him, "Under the rules of our country, you can go free."

Then they lead the Englishman to the guillotine. "Do you have any last words?"

He says, "God bless the Queen." They put him

on the block. And again the blade sticks and they let him go free.

Finally, they lead the German to the guillotine. "Your last words?"

He says, "You know, I think a little oil would keep that thing from sticking."

Vic is jumping up and down on a manhole cover, clapping his hands over his head and shouting with each leap, "Fifteen, fifteen . . ."

"What the hell are you doing?" asks a guy who is passing by.

"I am performing a very important service for the community. I learned this technique from a guru in India. I am ridding the world of stupidity."

"Really," says the guy, "let me try."

The man stands on the manhole cover and jumps up and down, saying, "Fifteen, fifteen . . ." As he is jumping Vic jerks the manhole cover away and the man drops into the sewer.

Vic puts the cover back on and starts jumping again, saying, "Sixteen, sixteen, sixteen . . ."

Ben is dying and his three sons are gathered around his deathbed. The first son says, "Dad, we'll have a big funeral when you're gone. There will be fifty limos and we'll spend a fortune on the flowers."

The second son says, "Let's just have a dozen cars for the family and we can get by with spending just a few hundred on the flowers."

The third son says, "Why spend any money? The relatives can use their own cars and we can ride in the hearse with Dad. I can pick some flowers out of the garden out back."

Ben raises his head from the pillow and says,

"Look, why not just hand me my pants and I'll walk to the cemetery?"

Paddy works on the docks and earns barely enough money to keep his wife and six kids going. One day he is loading a barge and he accidentally falls into the ocean and drowns. The insurance company presents the widow with a check for fifty thousand dollars.

At Paddy's wake, a friend approaches the new widow and says, "He was a fine man, pity he never learned to read or write."

"Nor to swim. Thank God."

A guy goes to the doctor complaining of terrible aches and pains. The doctor gives him a thorough work-up and sits the man down and says, "It doesn't look good. From what I can tell, you have an advanced case of herpes, a terrible rash, and syphilis. You also have German measles, poison oak, beriberi, pyorrhea, malaria, chicken pox, leprosy, not to mention sleeping sickness, typhus, diphtheria, and trench mouth."

"Doctor, what can I do?"

"We will place you in a special room in the hospital and feed you a special diet of pancakes and tortillas."

"And that will cure me?"

"No," says the doctor, "but it's the only food that we can slip under the door."

A widow is having a drink at her husband's favorite bar a few weeks after his funeral. The bartender is consoling her when he notices a new diamond ring on her hand.

"Did you buy yourself that ring with his insurance money?" he asks.

"John was so thoughtful," says the widow. "He left two thousand dollars for the burial and five thousand for a stone."

Bubba is applying for a job as a bouncer in a bar. The manager looks over his application and says to the guy, "You have been fired from every job that you've had."

"Yes, sir," says Bubba, "I'm no quitter."

In ancient times, a king condemns a man to die unless he can pass three tests. First, the man has to climb the sheer face of a tall mountain; second, he has to extract a sore tooth from an angry lion; and third, he has to get a kiss from a maiden who hates men.

With great effort, the man scales the mountain. Then he goes into a lion's den. Fierce growling emerges from the cave and the sound of gnashing teeth echos through the valley. After two hours, the man comes out of the cave with bruises and scratches all over him.

"Now," he says, "where's that lion that hates men?"

A little old lady is taking her first plane trip across the ocean when the pilot comes over the intercom with an announcement. "Ladies and gentlemen, our number-one engine has just failed, and we will be delayed about one hour."

A little bit later, the pilot makes another announcement. "Excuse me, folks, but our number-two engine has gone down, and we will be delayed about two hours."

Then the pilot comes over the intercom with another announcement. "I'm sorry to say that our number-three engine has just failed. We will be delayed three hours."

"My goodness," says the little old lady to the man next to her, "if that fourth engine goes, we'll be up here all night."

Leonard has been working late and is running to catch the last ferry home. Just as he gets to the pier he sees the ferry about ten feet from the shore. He takes a running leap and jumps on board the moving boat. He's lying battered and bruised on the deck and looks up at one of the crew members.

"I made it," says Leonard.

"I know," says the crew member. "Why didn't you wait? We were just pulling in to shore."

Three guys are sentenced to die by the firing squad. They bring the first guy out and stand him up against the wall.

They are just about to shoot him and the general gives the command. "Ready . . . aim . . ."

The guy thinks quick and yells out, "Earthquake!"

The firing squad runs for cover and the man escapes.

They bring out the second guy. Again the general gives the command, "Ready . . . aim . . ."

This time the man yells, "Flood!"

The firing squad panics again and the prisoner runs away.

Finally, they bring out the third prisoner, who has learned a lesson from the other two prisoners.

He's standing up against the wall when the general gives the command, "Ready . . . aim . . ."

The prisoner yells, "Fire."

It's the day before Thanksgiving and the butcher is just locking up when a man pounds on the door. "Please let me in," says the man, "I forgot to buy a turkey and my wife will kill me if I don't come home with one."

"Okay," says the butcher. "Let me see what's left." He goes into the freezer and discovers that there's only one scrawny turkey left. He brings it out to show the man.

"That one's too skinny. What else you got?" says the man.

The butcher takes the bird back into the freezer and waits a few minutes and brings the same turkey back out to the man.

"Oh, no," says the man, "that one doesn't look any better. You better give me both of them."

Ed is sentenced to die when he gets a last-minute call from his lawyer.

"I've got some good news and some bad news," says the lawyer.

"Tell me the bad news," says the convicted killer.

"They are going to send you to the electric chair at dawn."

"How can there be any good news?"

"I got the voltage reduced."

An ocean liner is out to sea when it strikes an iceberg and starts to sink. The passengers are getting into the wooden lifeboats. One guy takes an ax and starts to hack one of the boats into hundreds of pieces.

"What the hell are you doing?" yells the captain.

"Making a raft."

George, a local football star, is jogging down the street when he sees a building on fire. A lady is standing on a third-story ledge holding her pet dog in her arms.

"Hey, lady," yells George. "Throw me the dog."

"No," she cries, "it's too far."

"I play football, I can catch him."

The smoke is pouring from the windows, and finally, the woman waves to George, kisses her dog good-bye, and tosses the pup down to the street. George keeps his eye on the dog as it comes hurtling down toward him. The puppy bounces off an awning and George runs into the street to catch it. He jumps six feet into the air and makes a spectacular one-handed catch. The crowd that has gathered to watch breaks into cheers.

George does a little dance, lifts the puppy above his head, wiggles his knees back and forth, then spikes the dog into the pavement.

It's a terrible rainstorm and a prisoner is condemned to die by a firing squad. He is being led out to the field where he is to be shot and the wind is howling and it starts to hail. The men can barely see what's in front of them and the general says to the man, "Do you have any last words before you are shot?"

"Yes," he says. "There is no justice in this god-forsaken land. I should not die."

"Quit complaining," says one of the men, "we're the ones who have to walk back in this weather."

Old man Brewster goes to the funeral of his life-long friend Bill. He's just about to leave the funeral parlor when the mortician stops him and says, "Excuse me, sir, but may I ask how old you are?"

"I'm ninety-nine."

"Hardly worthwhile going home, is it?"

Patrick is on his deathbed. He can smell his wife cooking corned beef in the kitchen. Patrick gathers up all his strength and calls to her. "I know I haven't been able to eat these last few weeks, but that smells so good. I'd like to try just a bite."

"I'd like to give you some, but I'm saving it for the wake."

A battleship spots a light in the ocean and is on a collision course with it. The captain orders his radioman to send a signal, "Change your course ten degrees to the east."

The reply comes back. "Change your course ten degrees to the west."

Outraged, the captain sends this message: "I'm a captain in the United States Navy. Change your course."

"I'm a seaman second class, and you better turn your ship."

"I am a battleship ... get the hell out of the way!"

"Do what you want ... I'm a lighthouse."

Brian is walking in the mountains when the clouds part and God appears to him.

"God," he says, "I have always wanted to know. What is time like for You?"

"For Me," says God, "a hundred years is like one second."

"And God," says Brian, "what is money like to You?"

"A million dollars is like one penny to Me," answers God.

"God, would you give me a penny?" asks Brian. "In a second."

An American, an Israeli, and a Russian are in a plane crash and all of them die. They are at the Pearly Gates and St. Peter says to them, "Look, we're backed up right now. You can pay me a thousand dollars and be sent back to earth."

The American pays the money and is sent back to earth. One of his friends says to him, "What happened to the other two?"

"The Israeli bargained him down to $850. And the Russian was looking for two cosigners."

A guy is driving down the highway with his cat, his dog, and his horse in the trailer behind. They are forced off the highway by a truck coming full speed in the opposite direction. The man is thrown out of the truck and wakes up and sees a highway patrolman standing over his pet cat. The cop says, "A broken neck . . . poor kitty." He takes out his gun and puts the cat out of its misery. Then the cop sees the dog and says, "A broken back . . . poor dog." He shoots the dog. Then he walks over to the horse lying in the highway and says, "Three broken legs . . . poor horse." And again he takes out his gun and shoots the suffering horse.

Finally, the cop spots the man and walks over to him and says, "Are you okay?"

The man pulls himself up and says, "Never felt better in my life."

A customs agent is going through the luggage of an American who had just been to Paris. "I thought you said you had nothing but clothes," says the agent.

"That's right."

"Well," says the agent, holding up a bottle of expensive cognac, "what do you call this?"

"That's my nightcap."

An old man carrying a huge suitcase gets on a train that's headed for Los Angeles. The conductor comes around and asks him his destination.

"Los Angeles," says the old man.

"That'll be forty-five dollars," says the conductor.

"I'll give you twenty," says the old man.

"Sorry, but the fare is forty-five," says the conductor.

"Twenty dollars is my top offer," says the old man.

"Look, mister," says the conductor, "I don't have time to play games. The fare is forty-five."

"What about the senior-citizen discount?"

"That *is* the discount," says the conductor, "forty-five dollars."

"I won't pay it," says the stubborn old man.

The conductor is at the end of his rope. The train is going over a bridge that runs over a river. He takes the suitcase and threatens the old man: "If you don't pay, I'll throw this into the river."

"Not only are you trying to take all my money," says the old man, "but now you're going to drown my poor innocent wife."

A man is on vacation in a remote beach in Florida. He's sitting on the beach on a hot sunny day and asks one of the locals who comes walking by, "Are there any alligators in the water?"

"No, I've never seen an alligator in these parts."

"That's great," says the guy, and runs into the water. He is swimming and splashing about and the local man is just standing on the shore watching him.

"The reason there's no alligators," yells the local from the shore, "is because they are afraid of the sharks."

An anthropologist flies to deepest Africa to do research on a tribe of cannibals. He meets with the chief of the tribe and the chief agrees to answer his questions. The cannibals are just about to eat dinner. The chief says, "Tonight we are feasting on leg of warrior. Brave warriors are rare in these parts, so we eat them a little at a time." The anthropologist notes this in his logbook.

The next day the cannibals are sitting down to lunch. The chief says, "We are eating a stew made from a group of Club Med tourists. Tourists are plentiful in the summertime." The anthropologist writes this in his notes.

"Chief," asks the anthropologist, "what do you eat if you want something special?"

"I like heart of lawyer, but I haven't had it in years."

"Not many lawyers around here?"

"It's not that," says the chief. "Do you know how many lawyers we have to kill before we find one with a heart?"

Three men are at the Pearly Gates waiting for St. Peter to interview them. The first man steps forward. St. Peter says, "How did you die?"

"Well," says the man, "I was jogging down the street when *wham*! a refrigerator fell out of a second-story window, and next thing you know, here I am."

"You can enter heaven," says St. Peter. "Next."

The second man comes forward. "And how did you meet your end?"

"I suspected that my wife was having an affair, so I came home early from work. I could hear them in the apartment when I was unlocking the front door. But when I got inside, I couldn't find the guy anywhere. I looked out the window and I saw him running away, so I pushed the refrigerator out the window and it landed right on him. Unfortunately, my wife was so mad she pushed me out the window."

"This is a difficult case," says St. Peter, "but you have a good record otherwise, so I'll let you in."

Finally, it is the third man's turn to be interviewed. St. Peter looks at him and says, "And how did you die?"

"Well, St. Pete, I was sitting in a refrigerator minding my own business. . . ."

PLUME (0452)

RIB-TICKLING BOOKS

☐ **THE UNOFFICIAL DENTIST'S HANDBOOK by Candy Schulman with illustrations by Ian Ross.** More laughs than nitrous-oxide—this hilarious book, brimming with outrageous illustrations, makes an ideal gift for every practitioner and every patient who has trouble understanding what's so funny about oral surgery. (265959—$7.95)

☐ **THE UNOFFICIAL MOTHER'S HANDBOOK by Norma and Art Peterson.** The essential guide for the only person who ever applauded when you went to the bathroom; the adjudicator of who hit whom first; the person known to begin sentences with "You'll be sorry when . . ." Here is an affectionately funny survey of motherhood from "day 1" through "leaving the nest" and "are you back again?" (262461—$6.95)

☐ **THE JOYS OF YINGLISH by Leo Rosten.** "What a book! A celebration of scholarship, humor and linguistic anthropology." —William F. Buckley, Jr. "Open it anywhere for a laugh. Or start with *abracadabra* and work through *zlob* for an education and endless amusement."—*Booklist* (265436—$14.95)

Prices slightly higher in Canada.

There's an epidemic with 27 million victims. And no visible symptoms.

It's an epidemic of people who can't read.

Believe it or not, 27 million Americans are functionally illiterate, about one adult in five.

The solution to this problem is you... when you join the fight against illiteracy. So call the Coalition for Literacy at toll-free **1-800-228-8813** and volunteer.

Volunteer Against Illiteracy. The only degree you need is a degree of caring.